Kitten Color Journey:

Relax and Purr with Cat Lovers

Coloring Book

Corinne Larsen

Cover Art by Arjane Kinney

Kitten Color Journey:

Relax and Purr with Cat Lovers

Larsen Falls Publishing

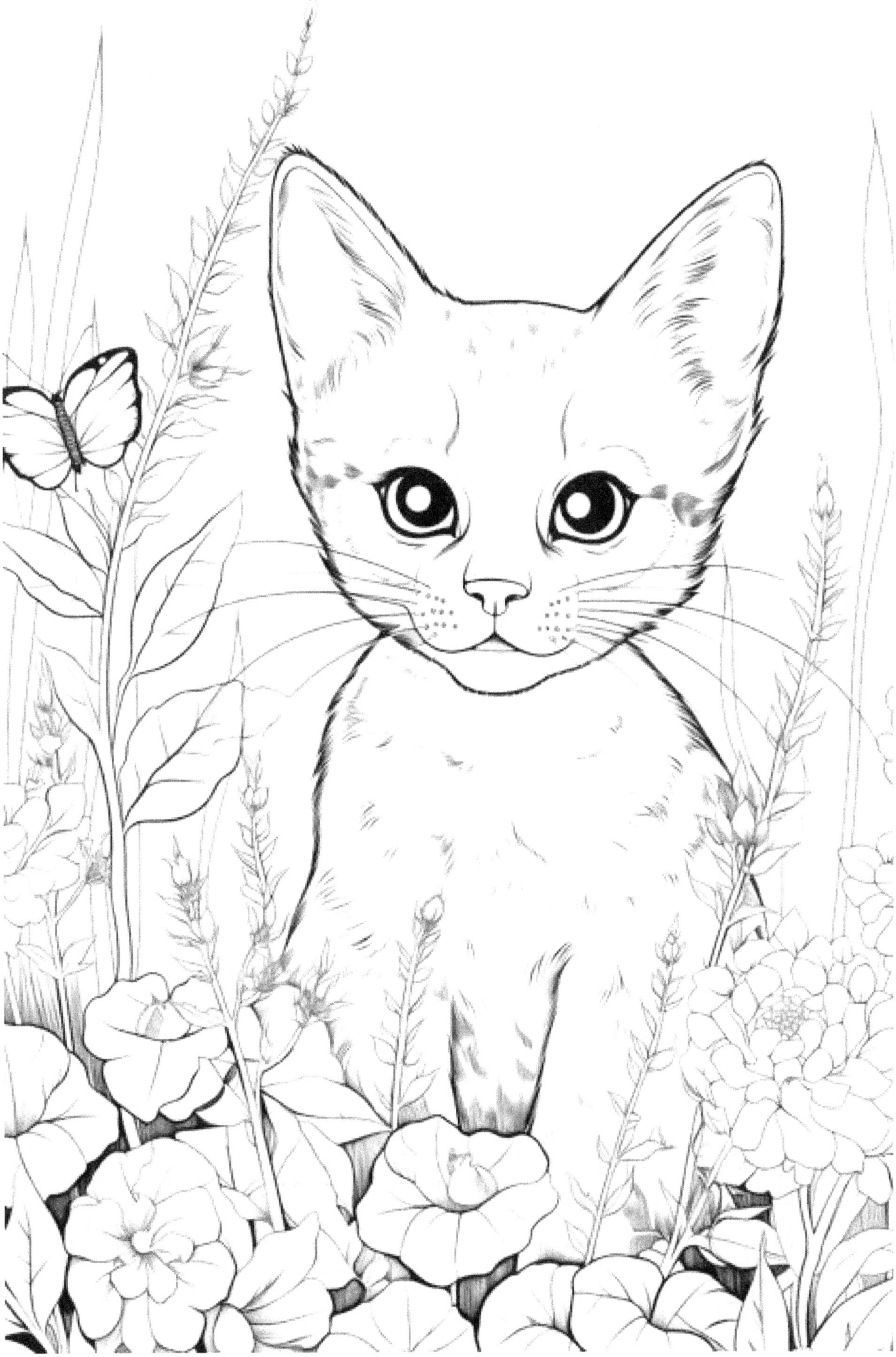

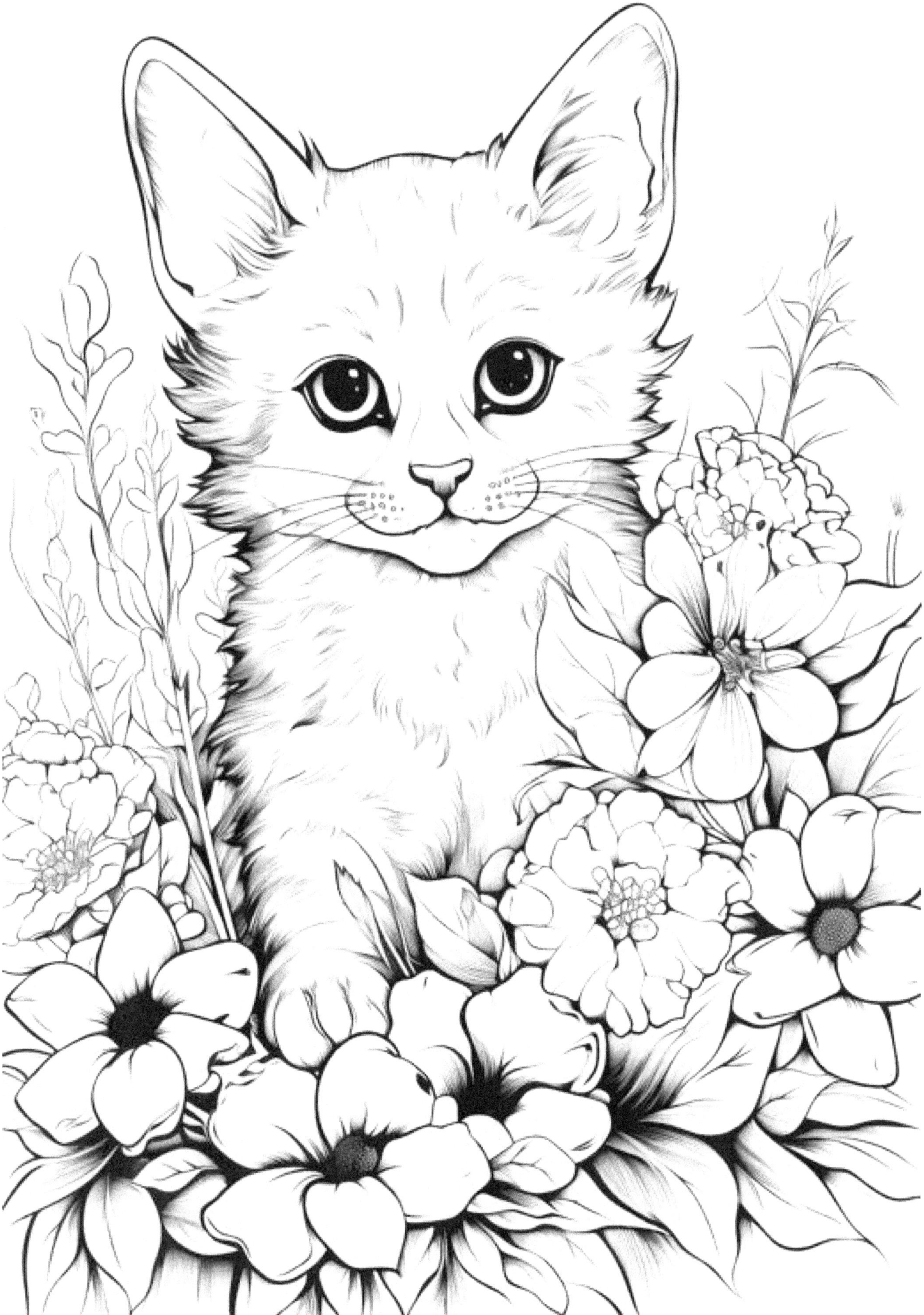

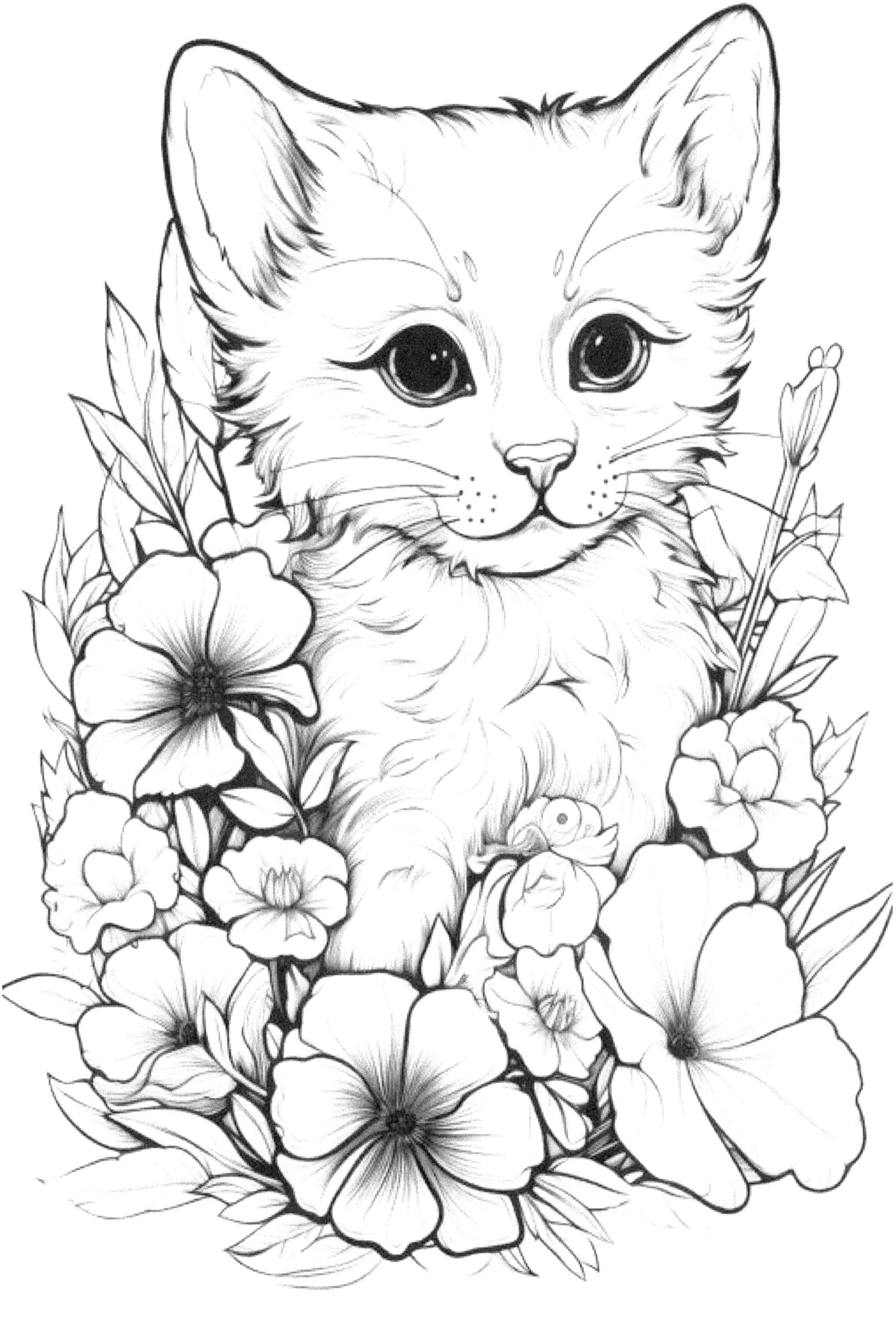

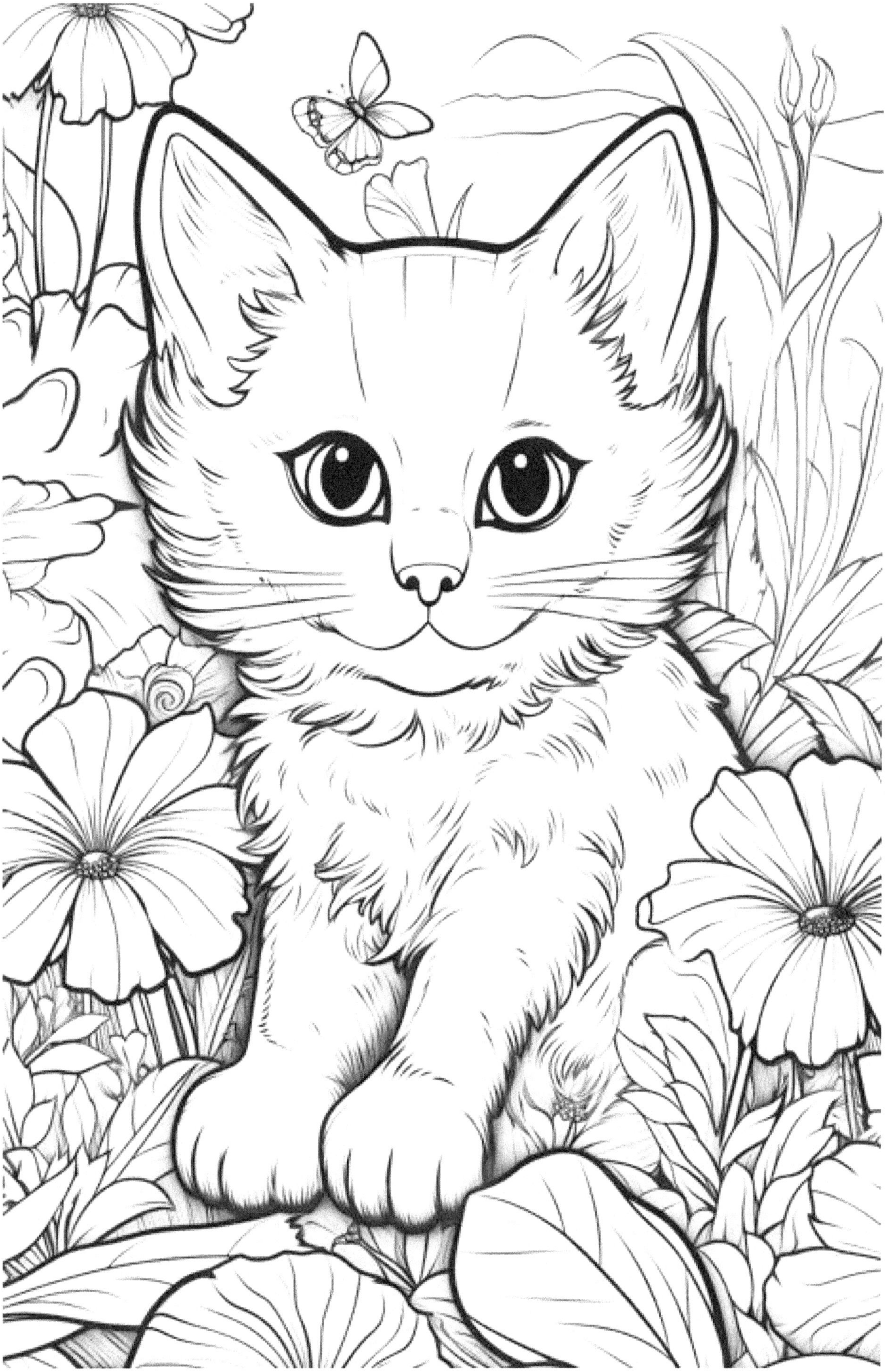

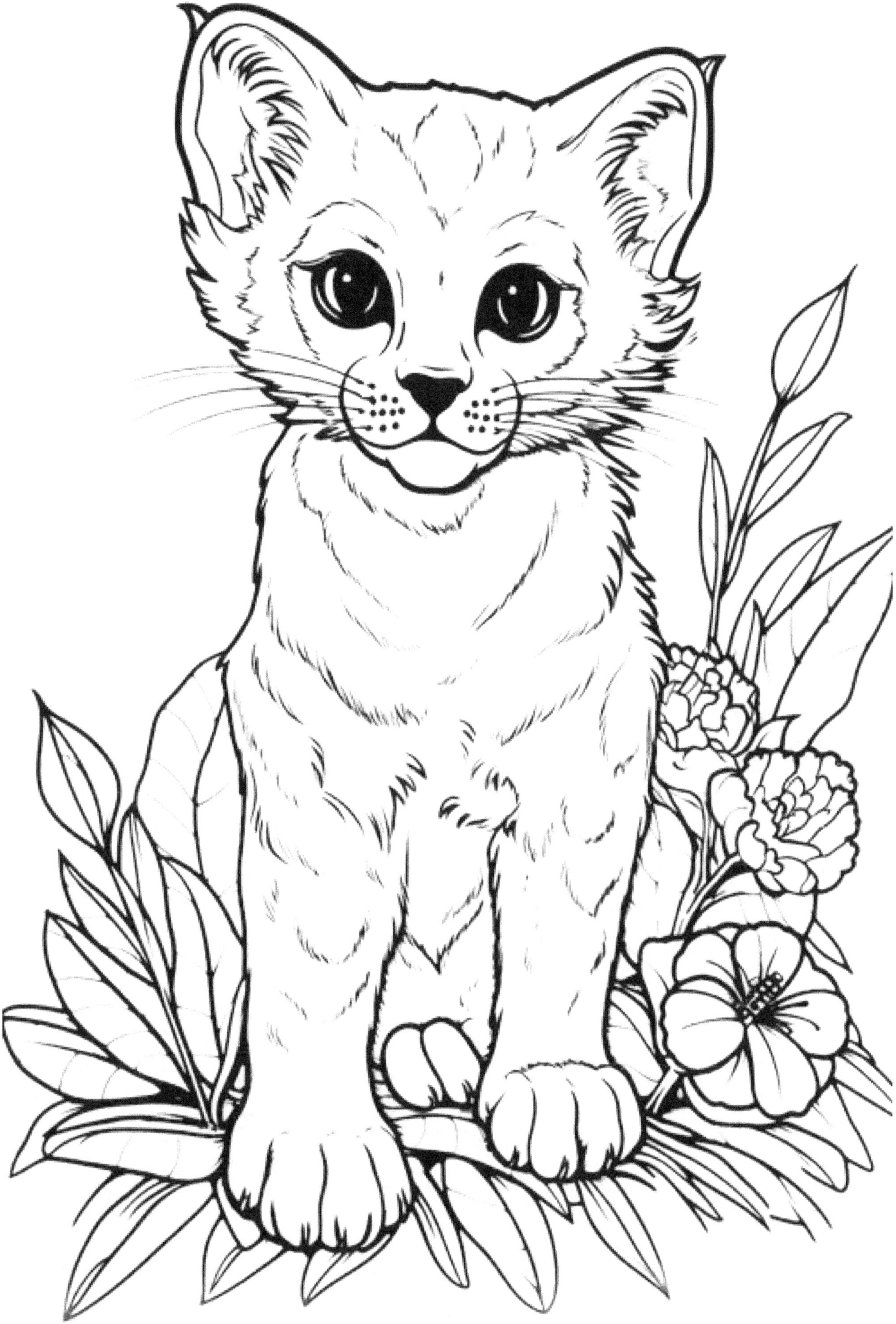

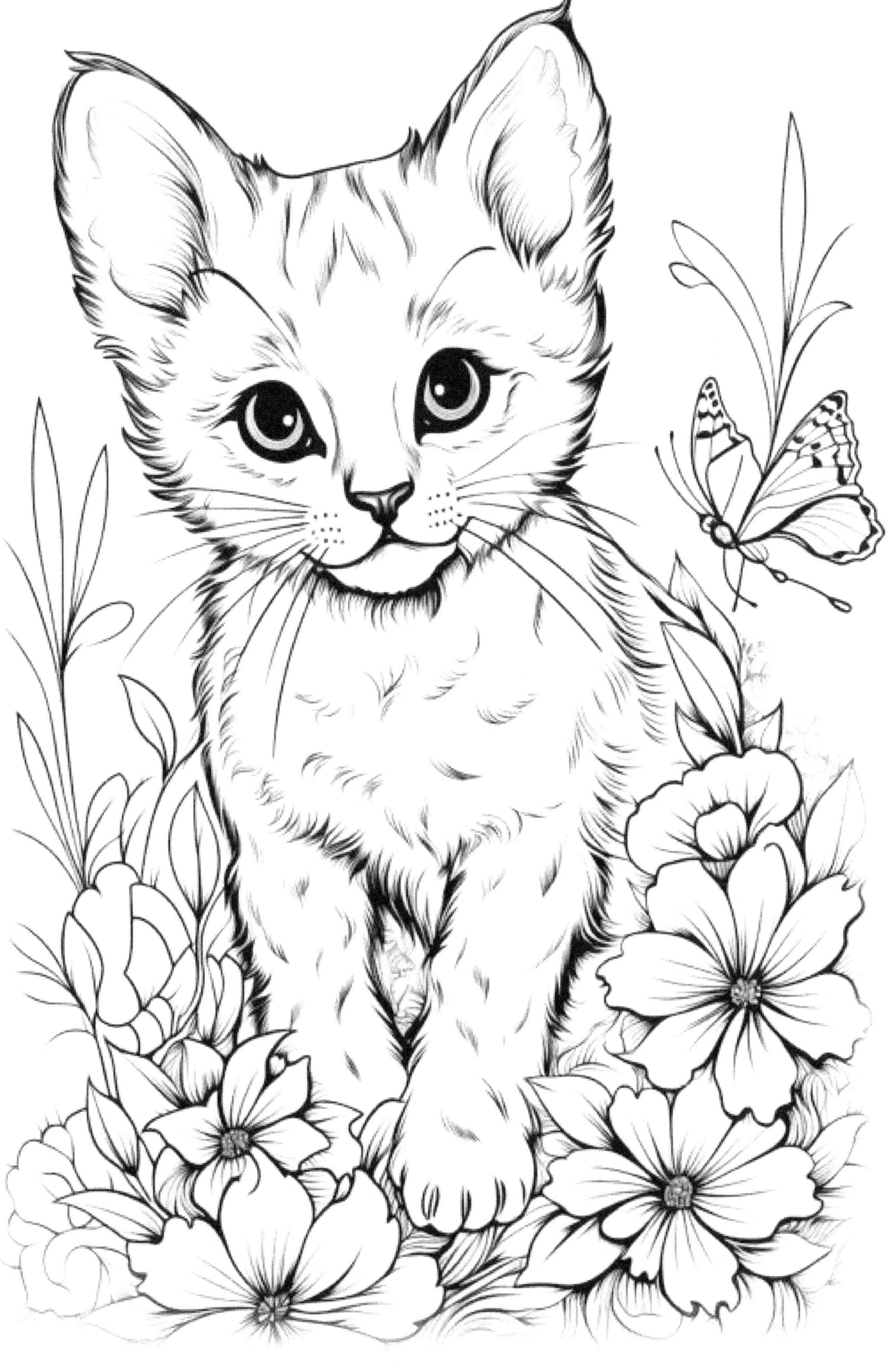

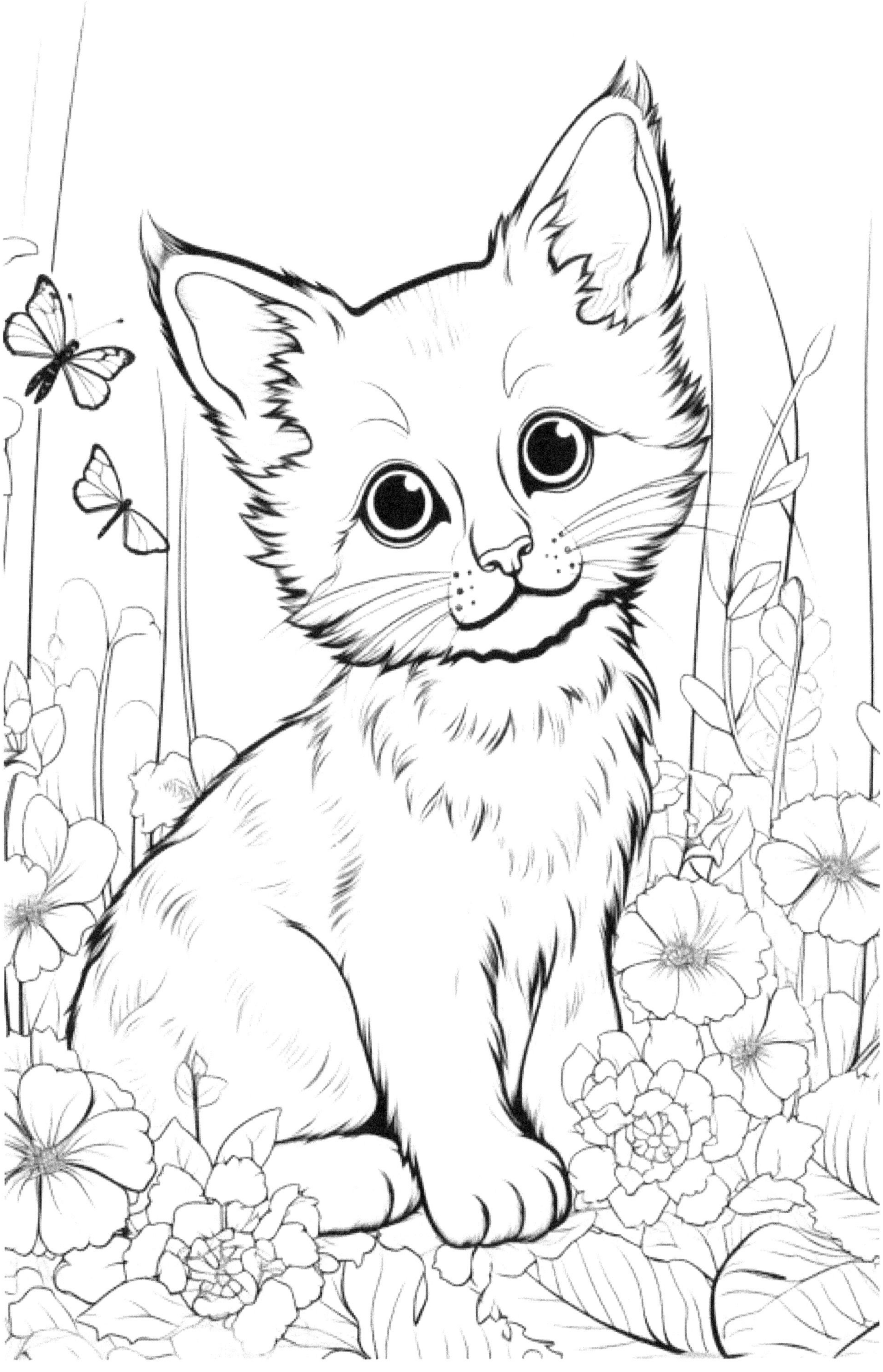

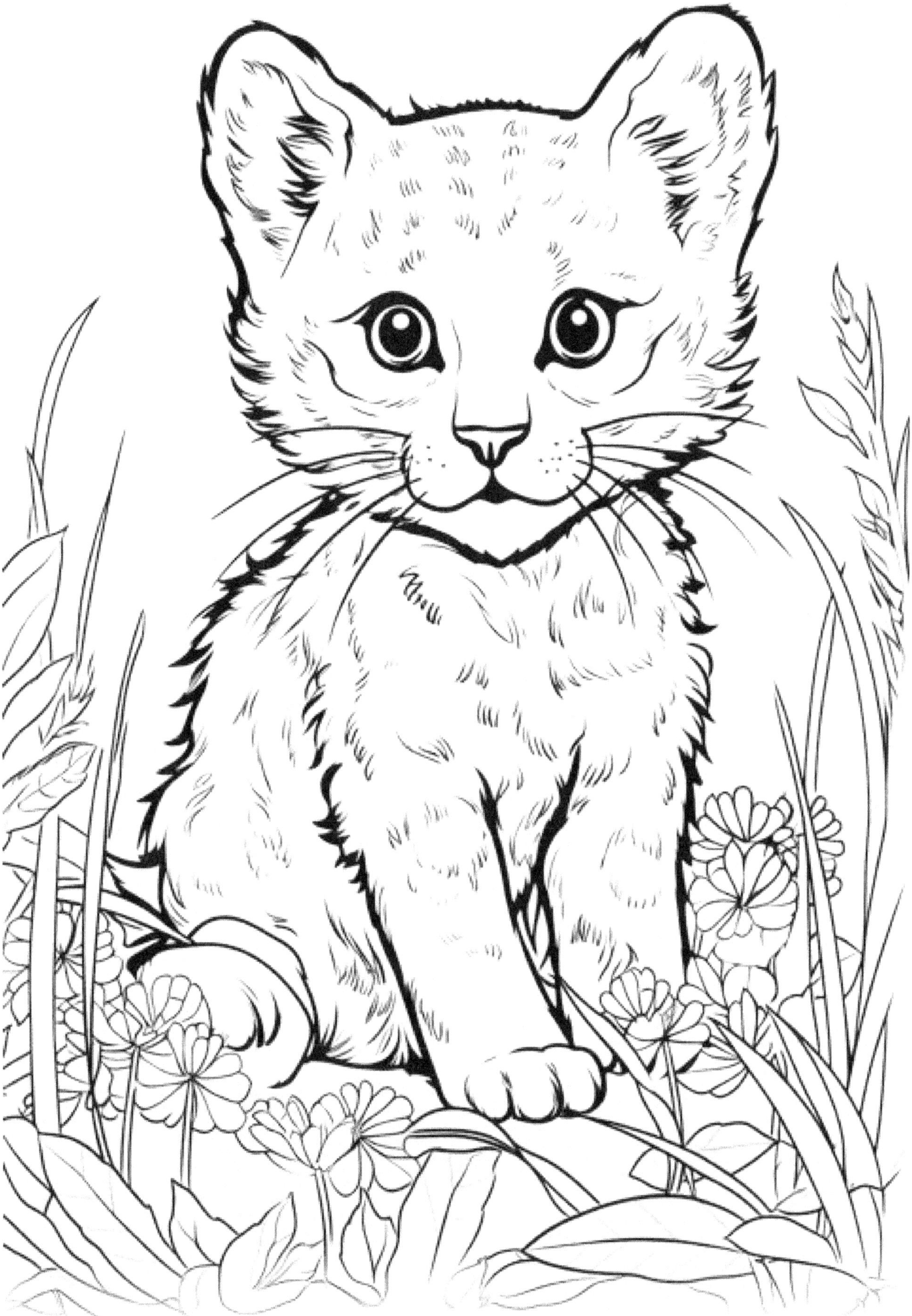

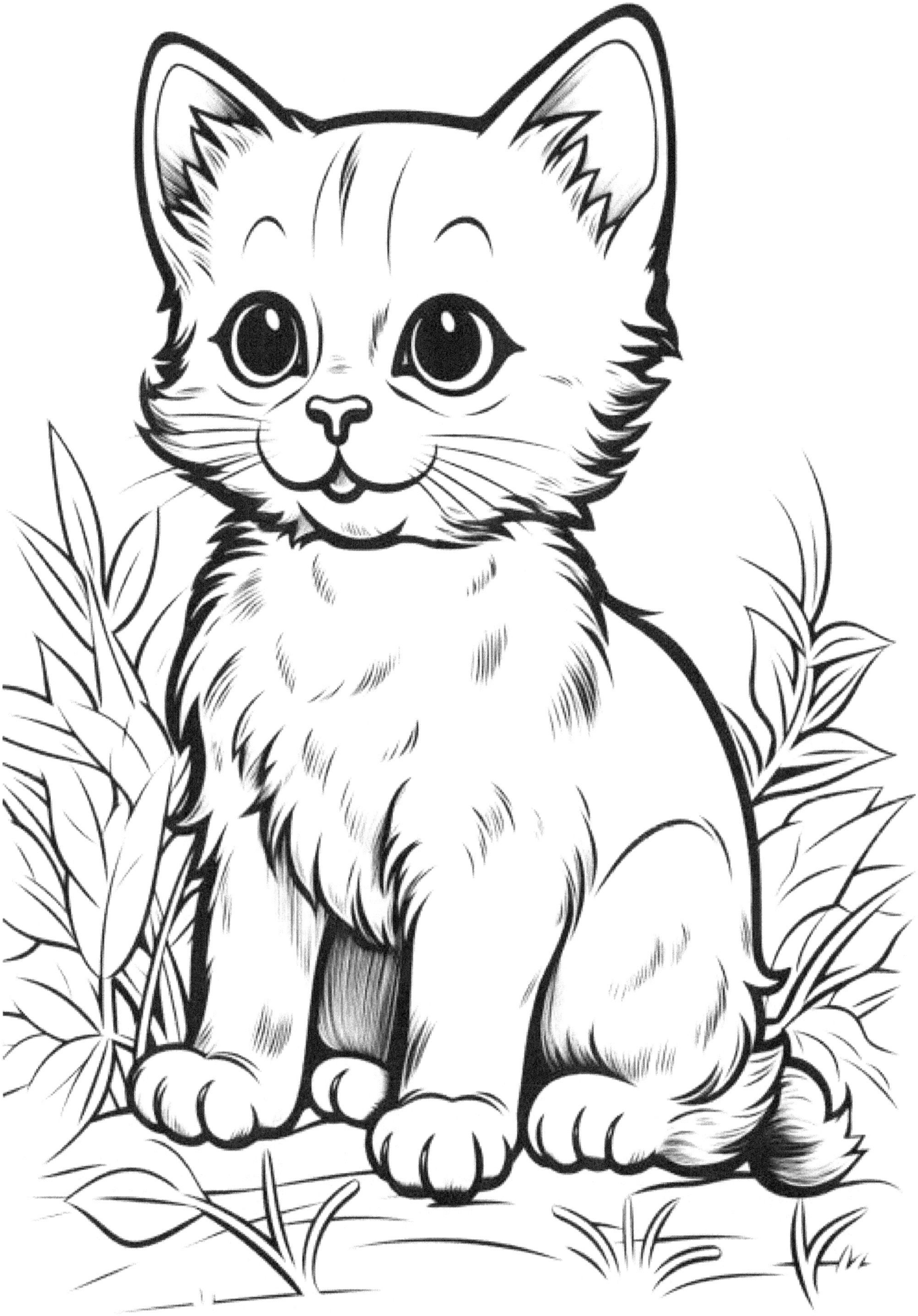

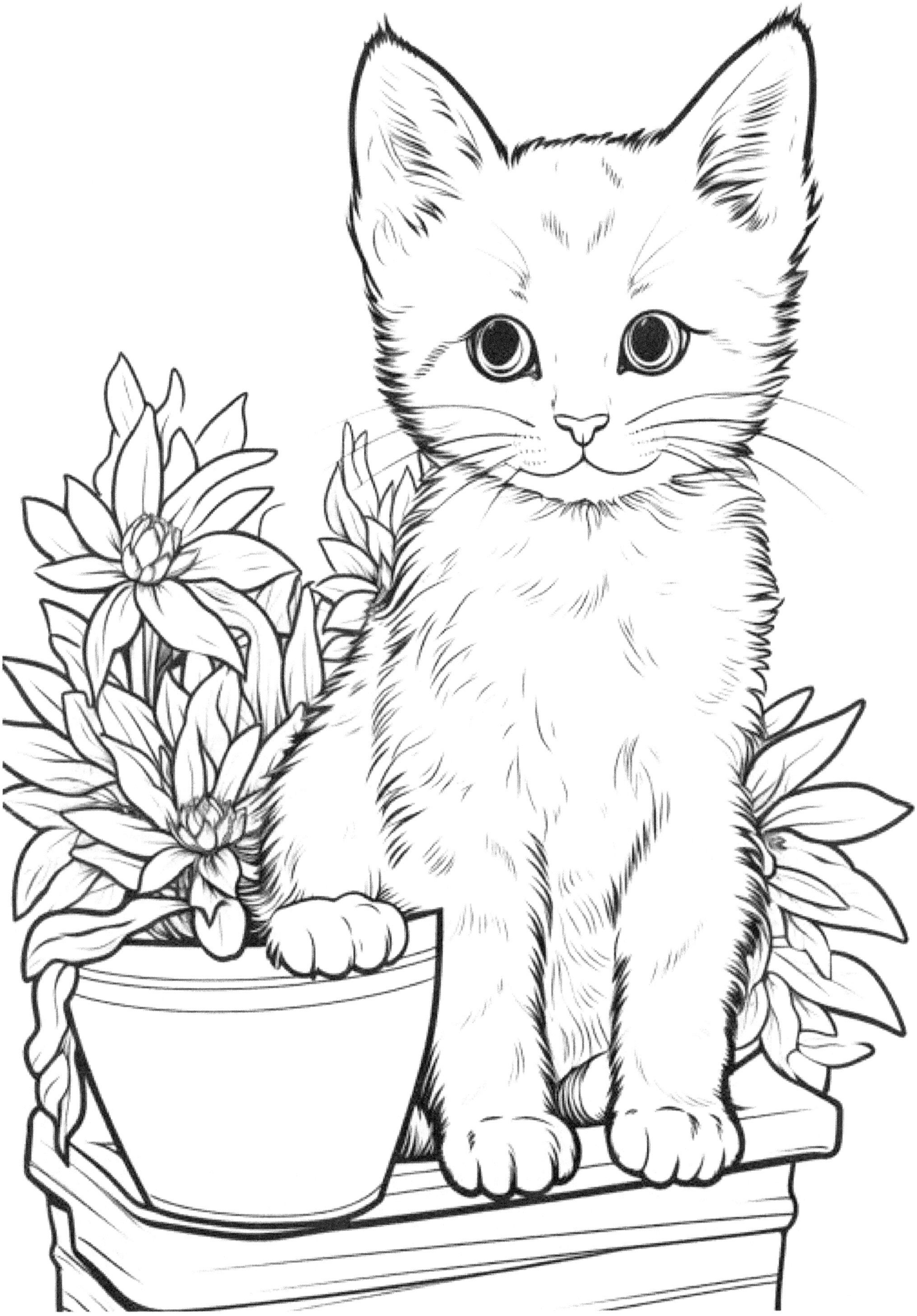

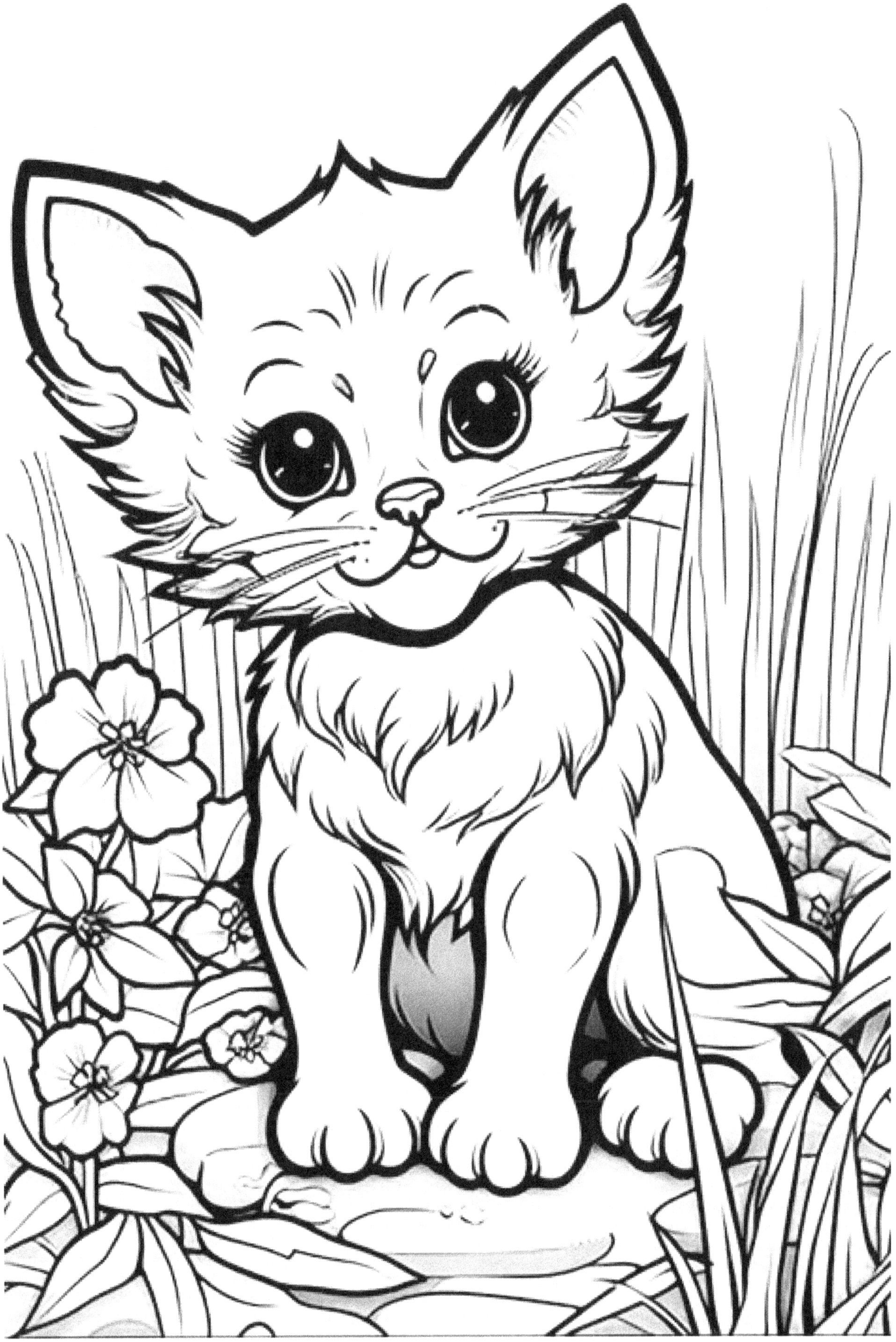

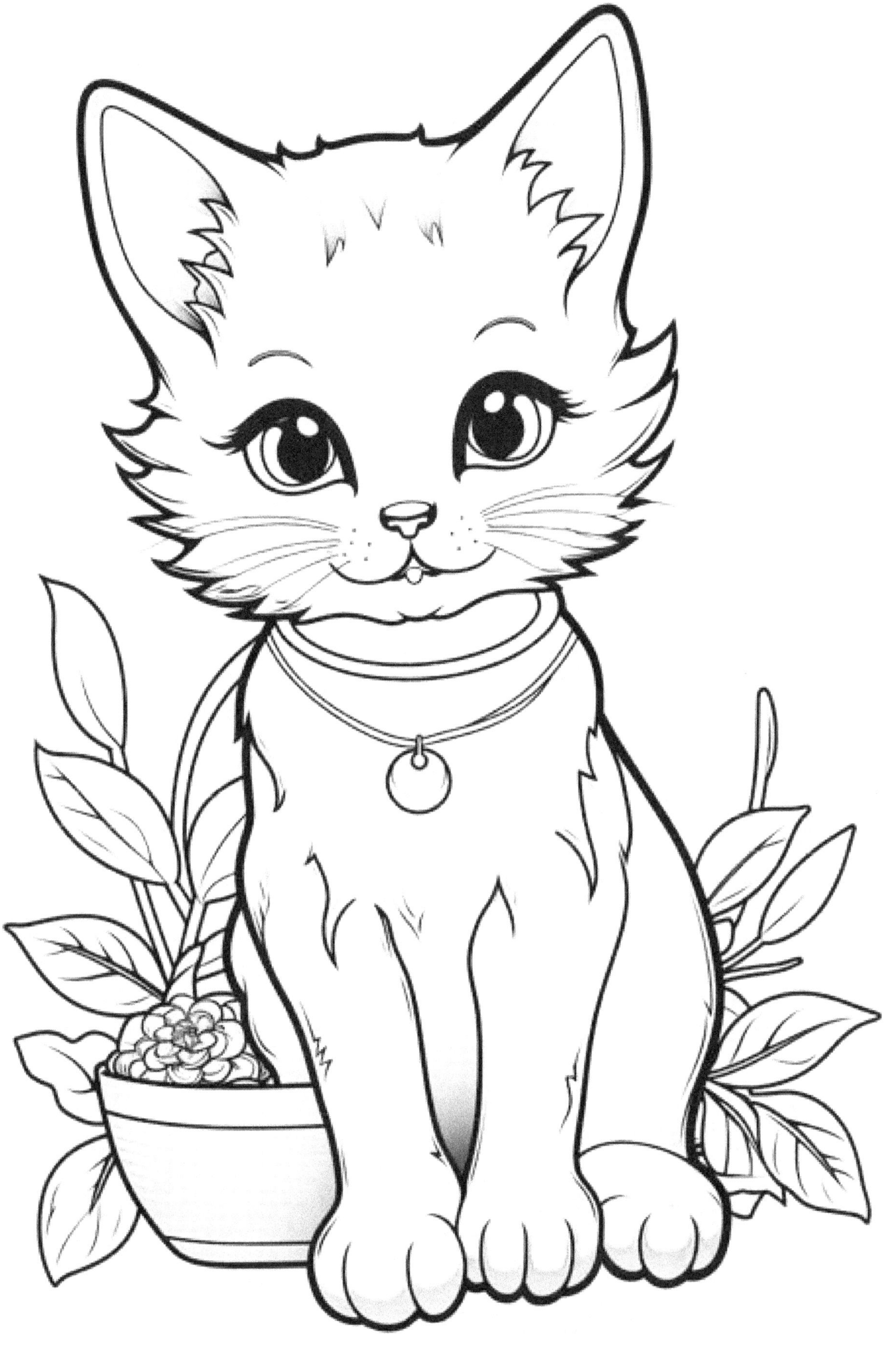

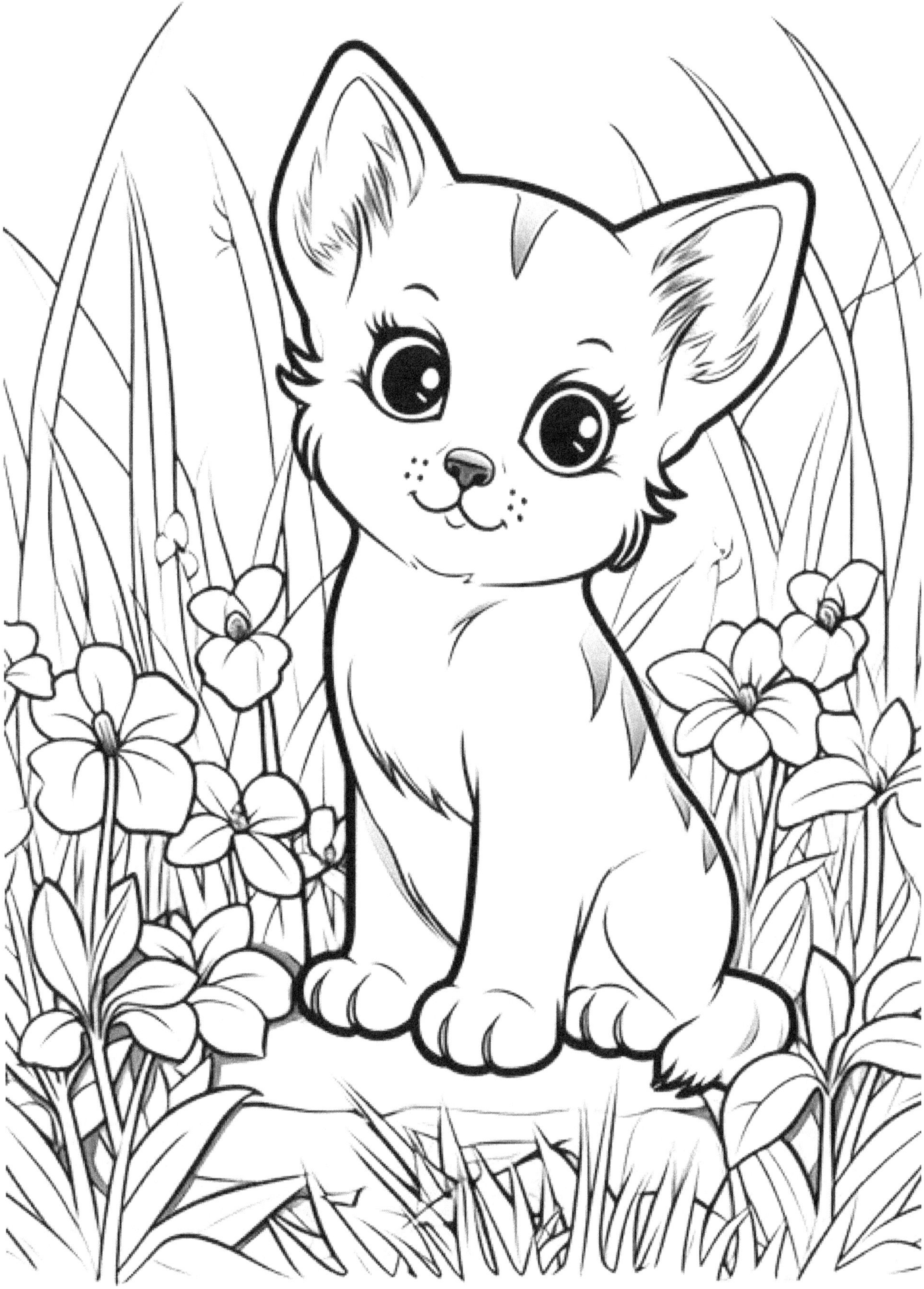

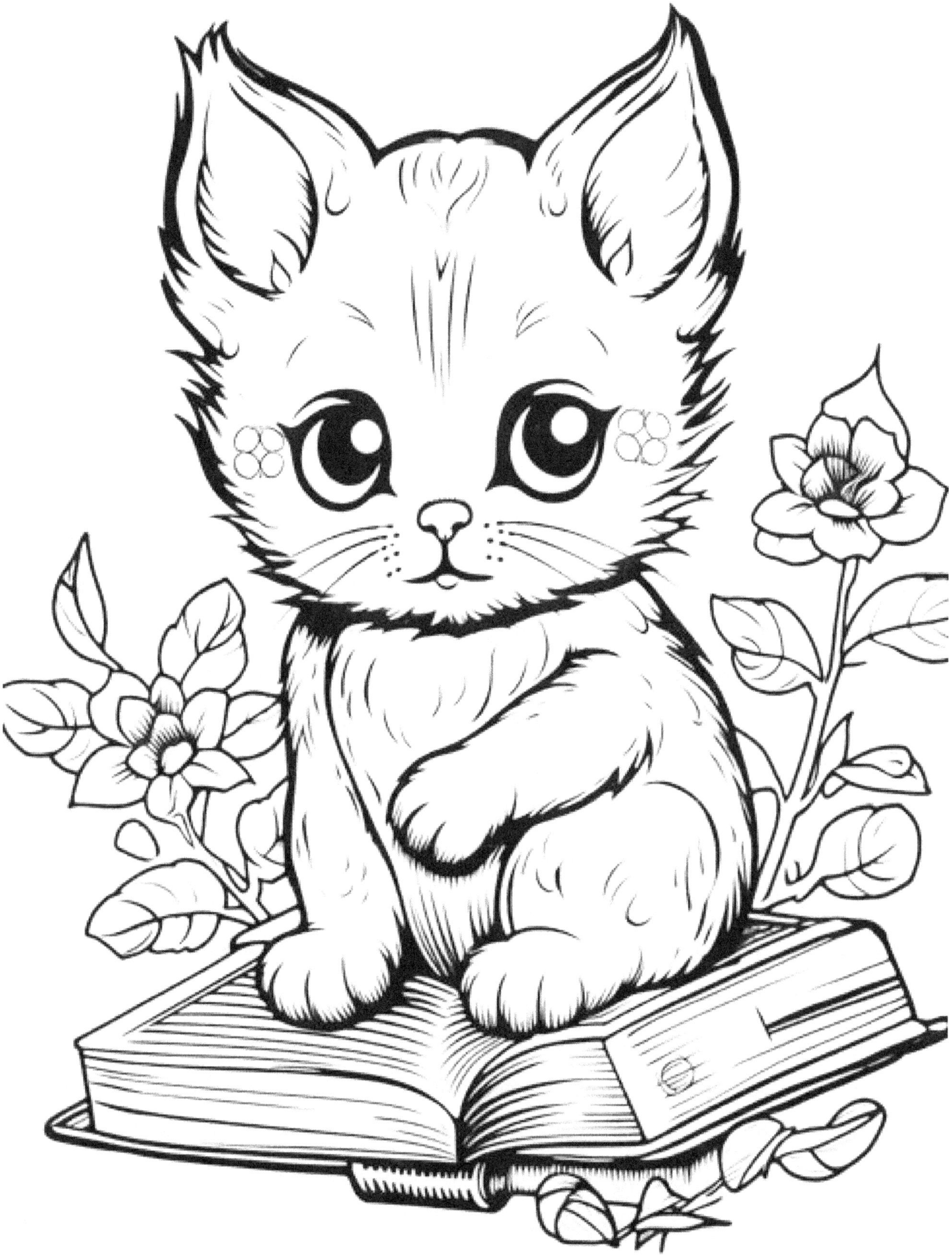

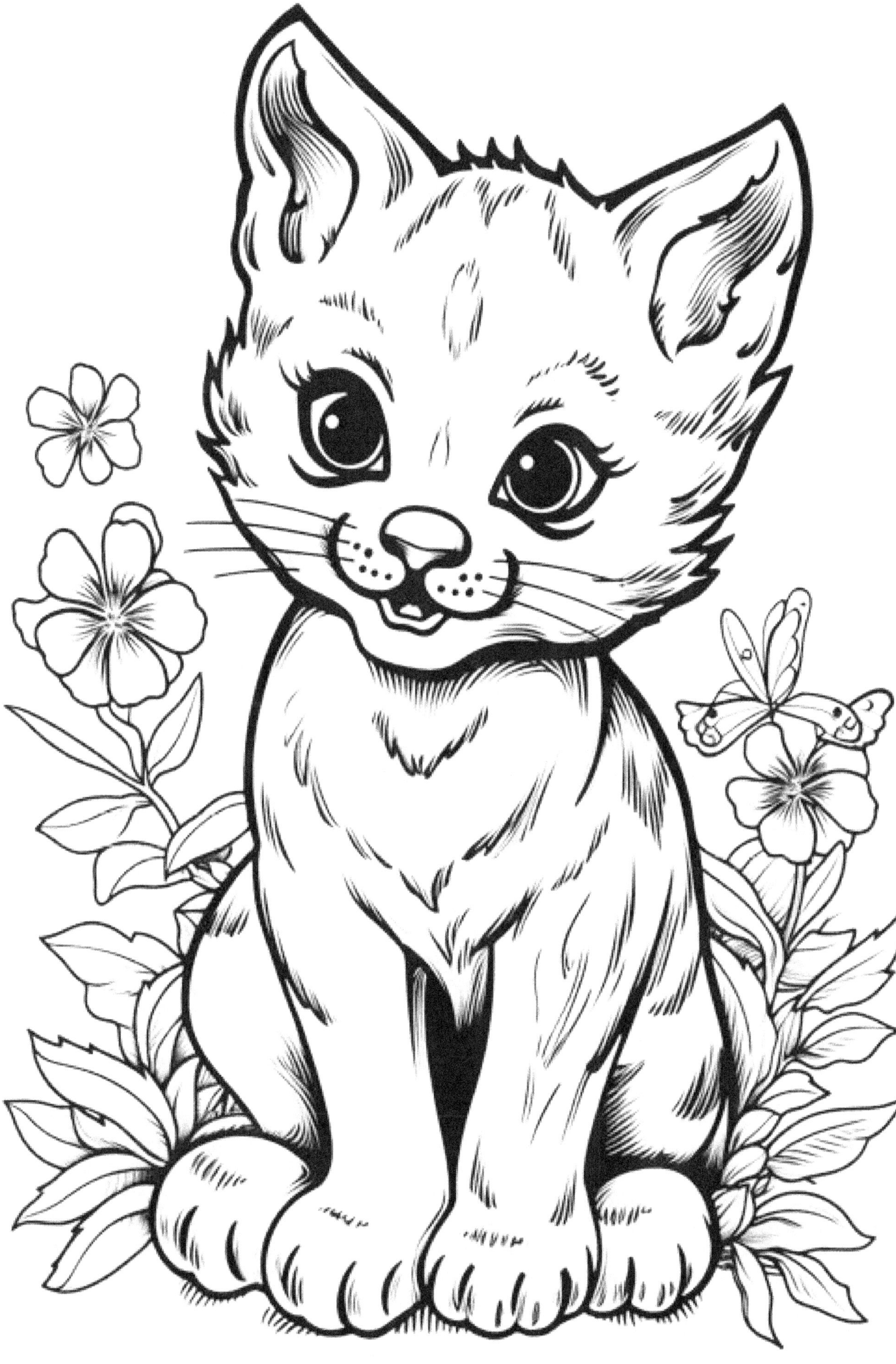

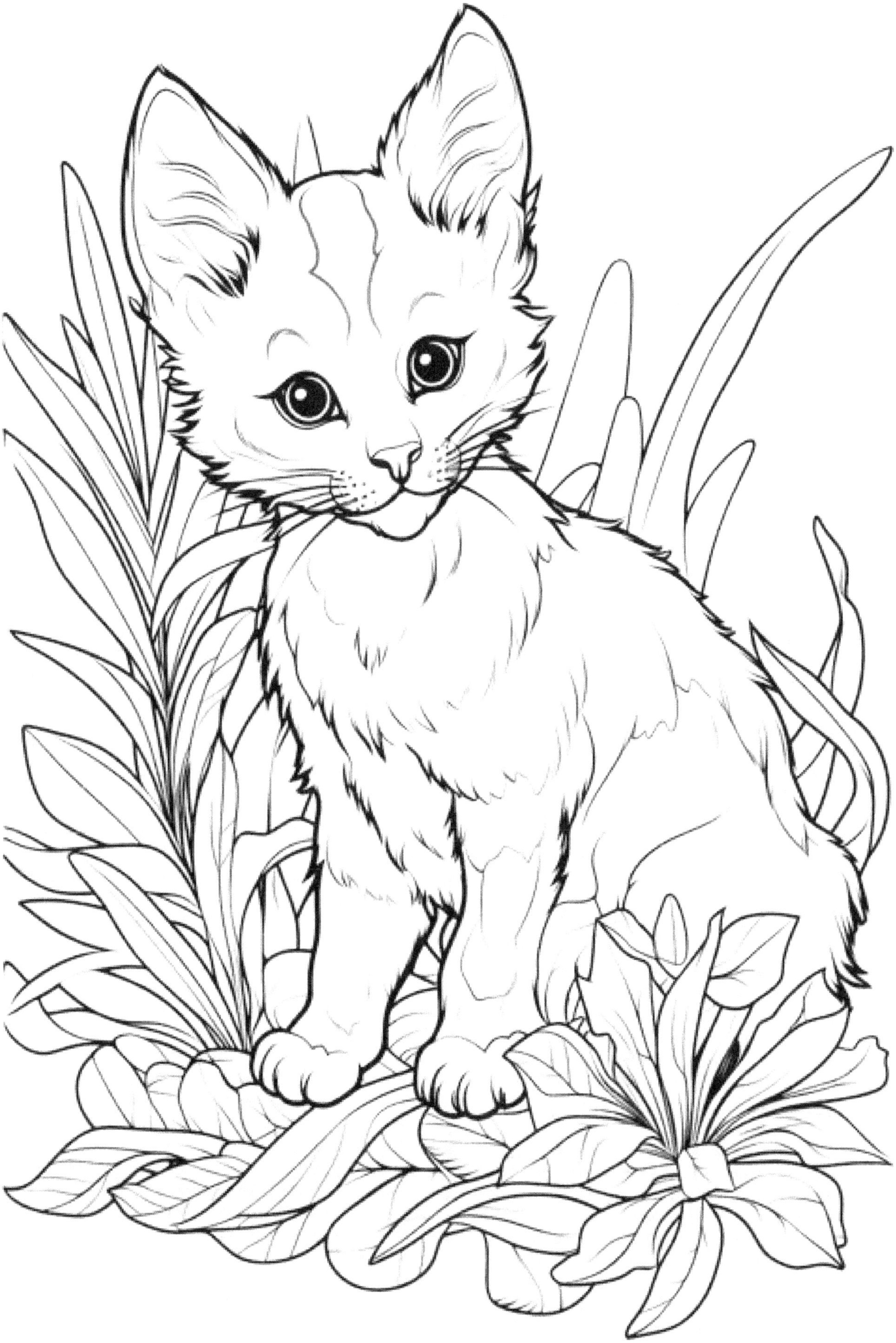

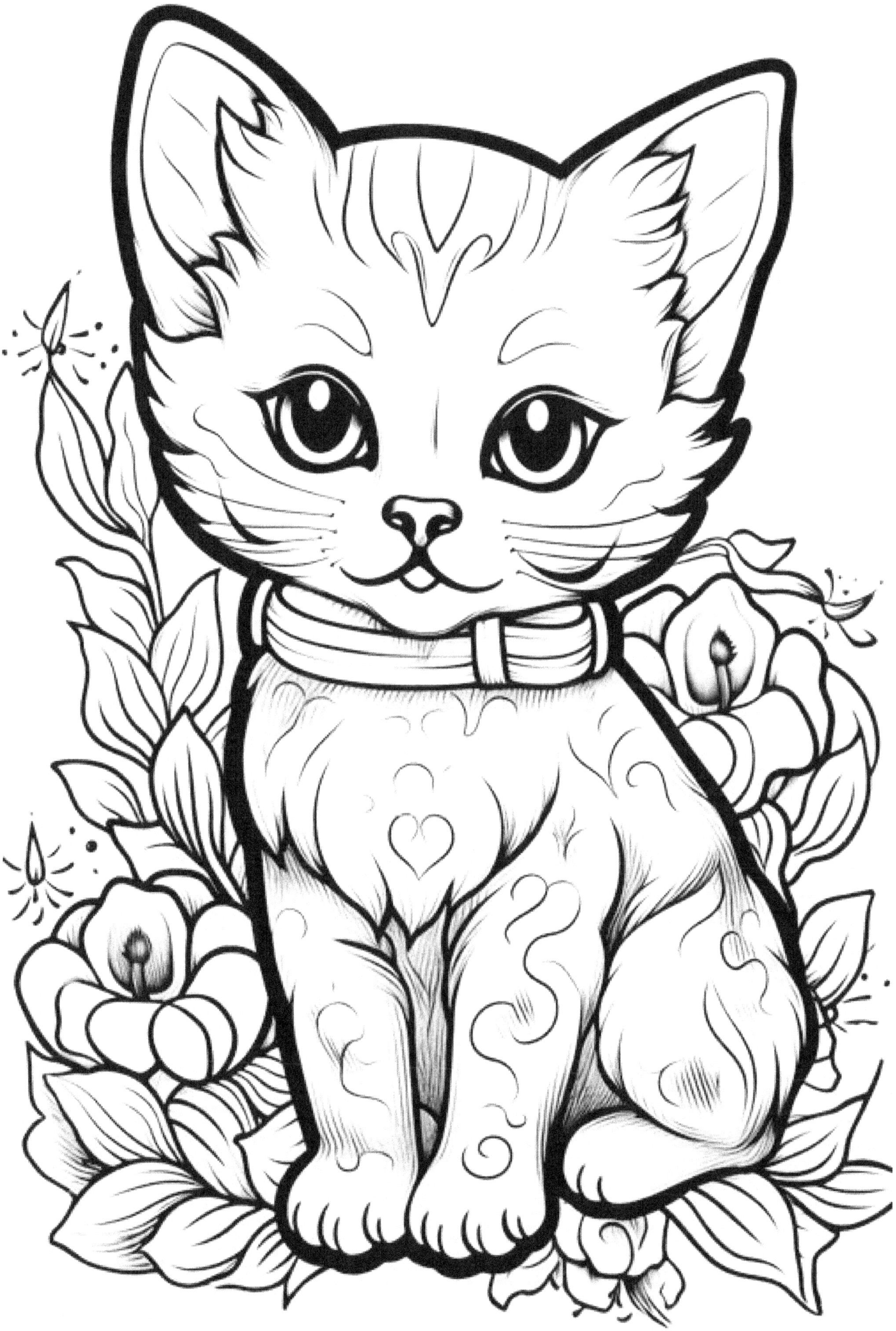

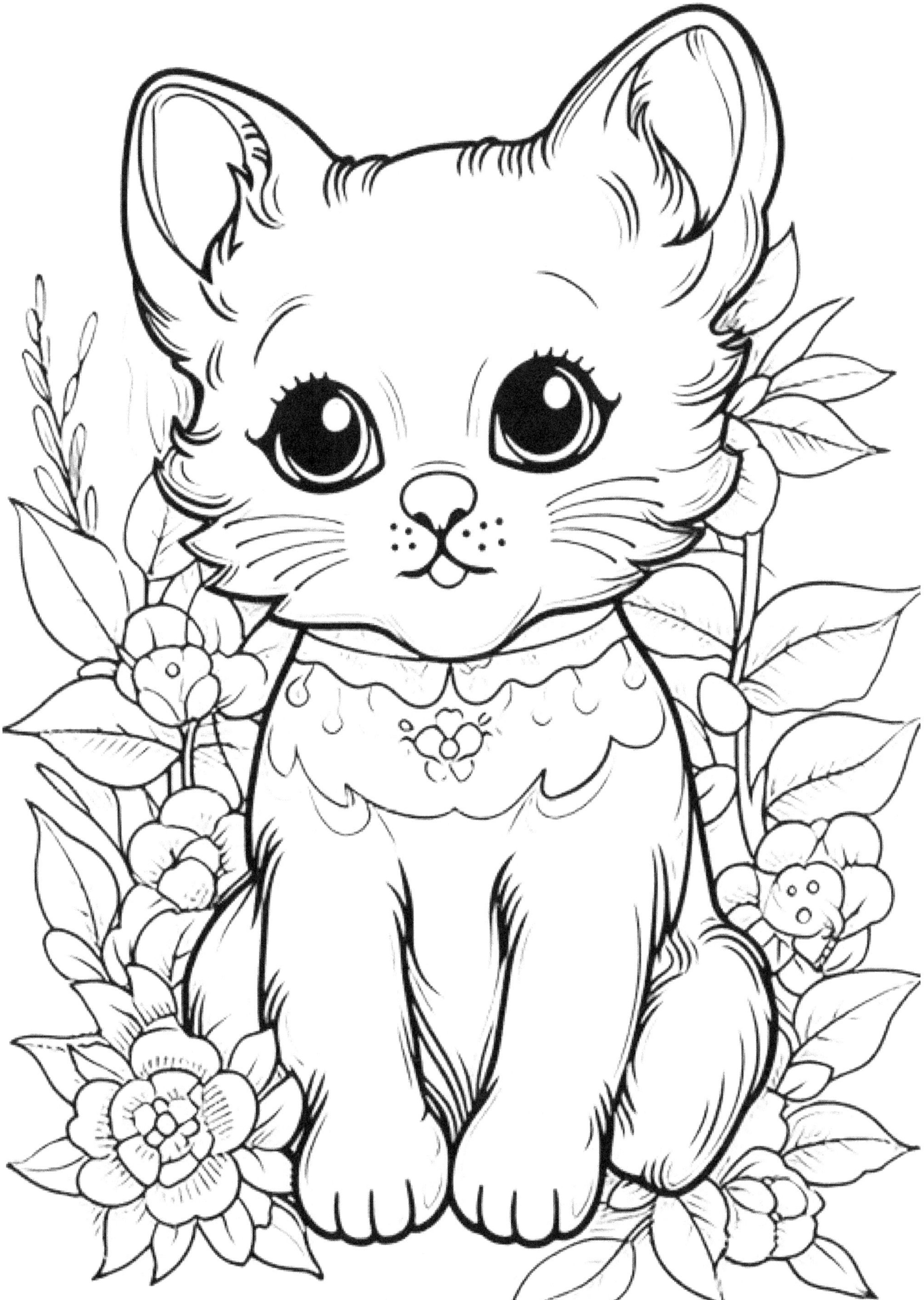

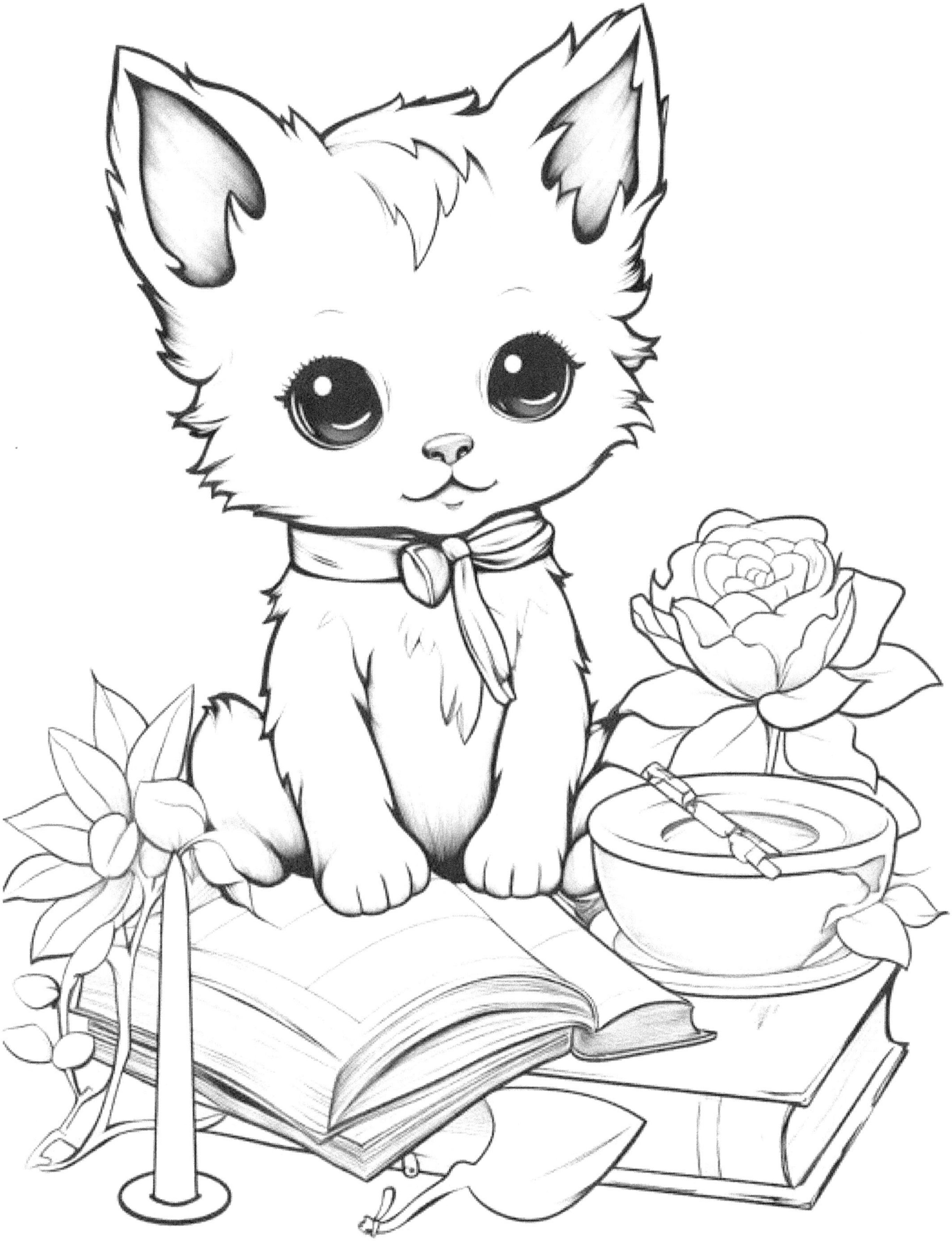

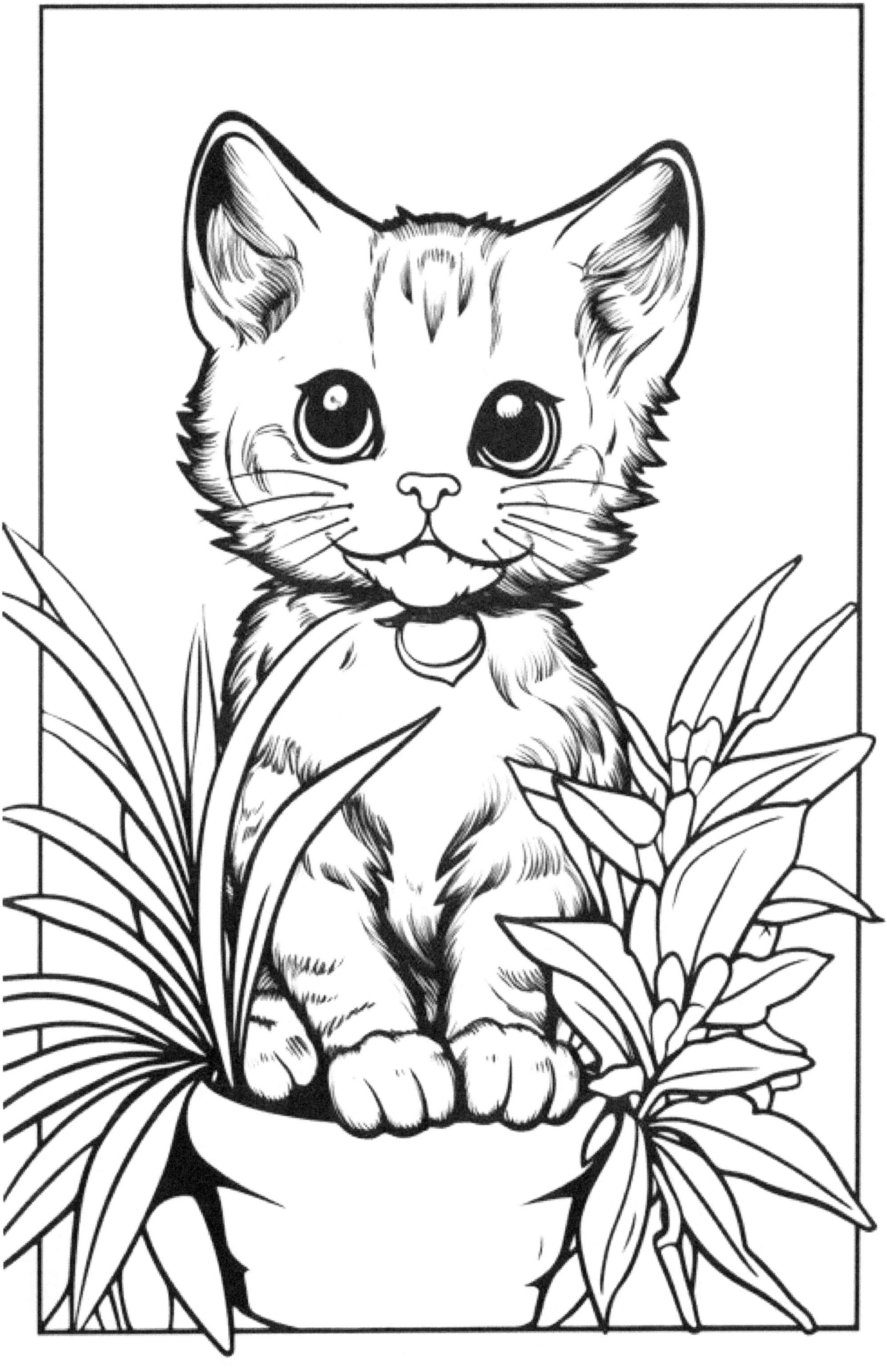

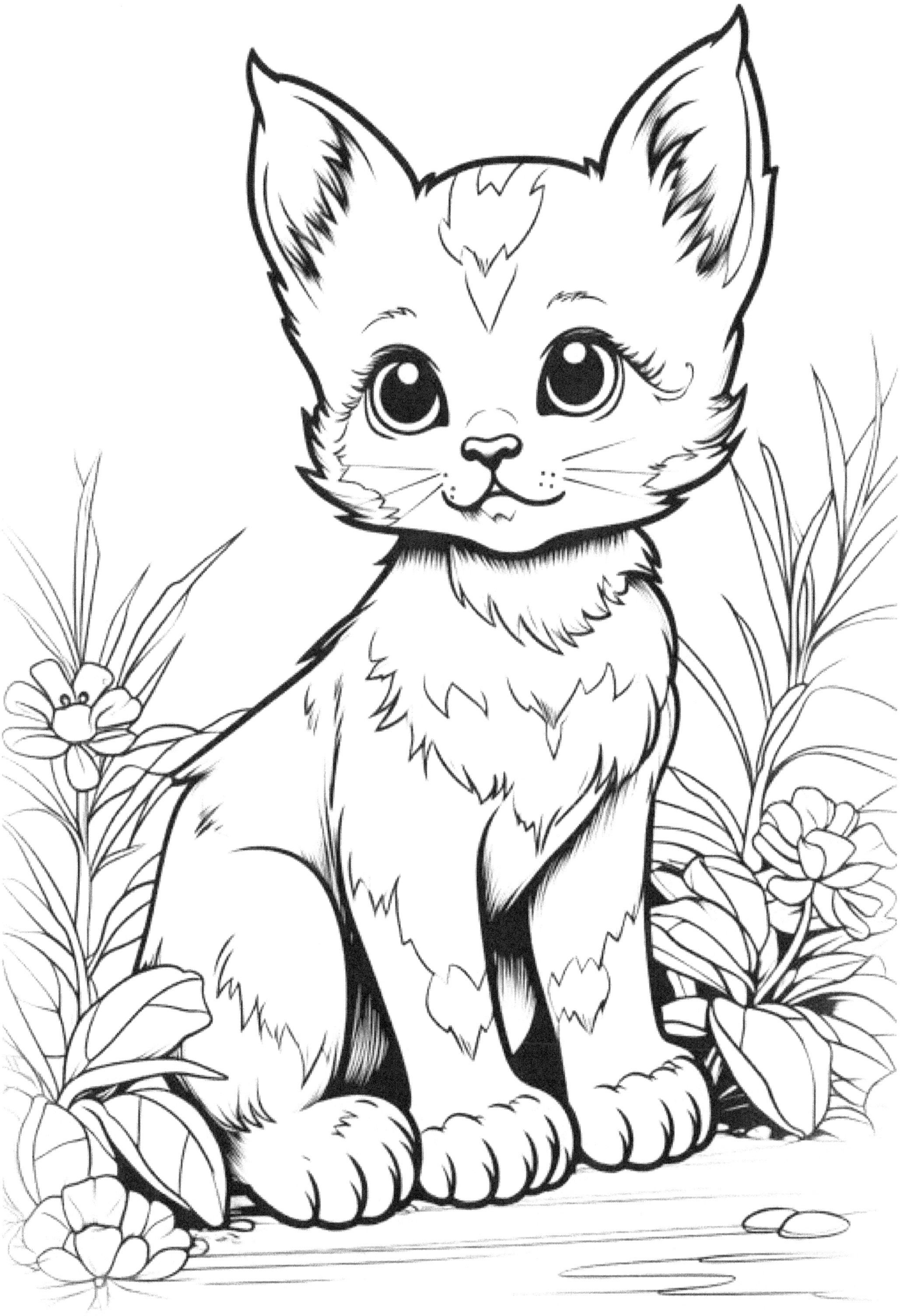

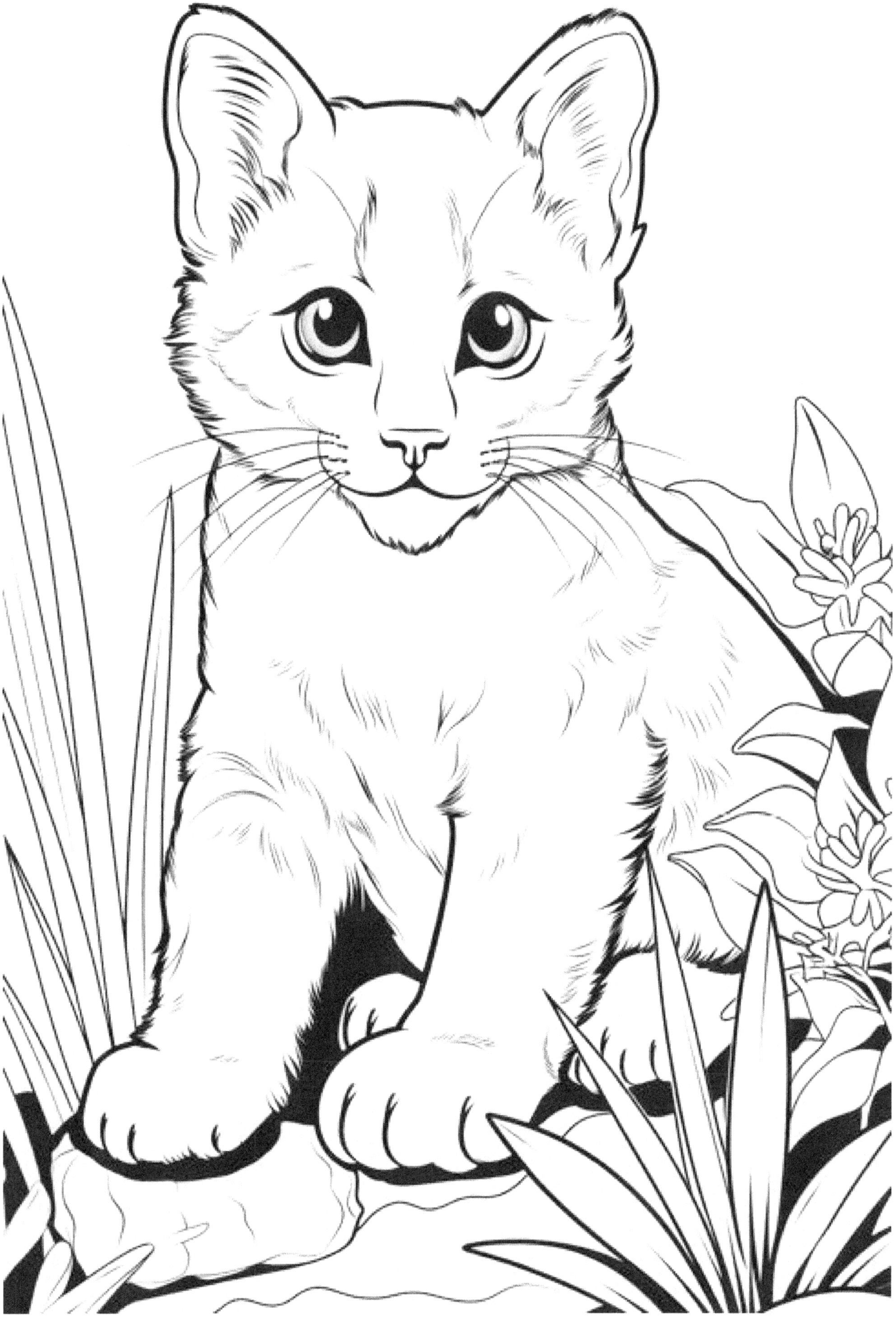

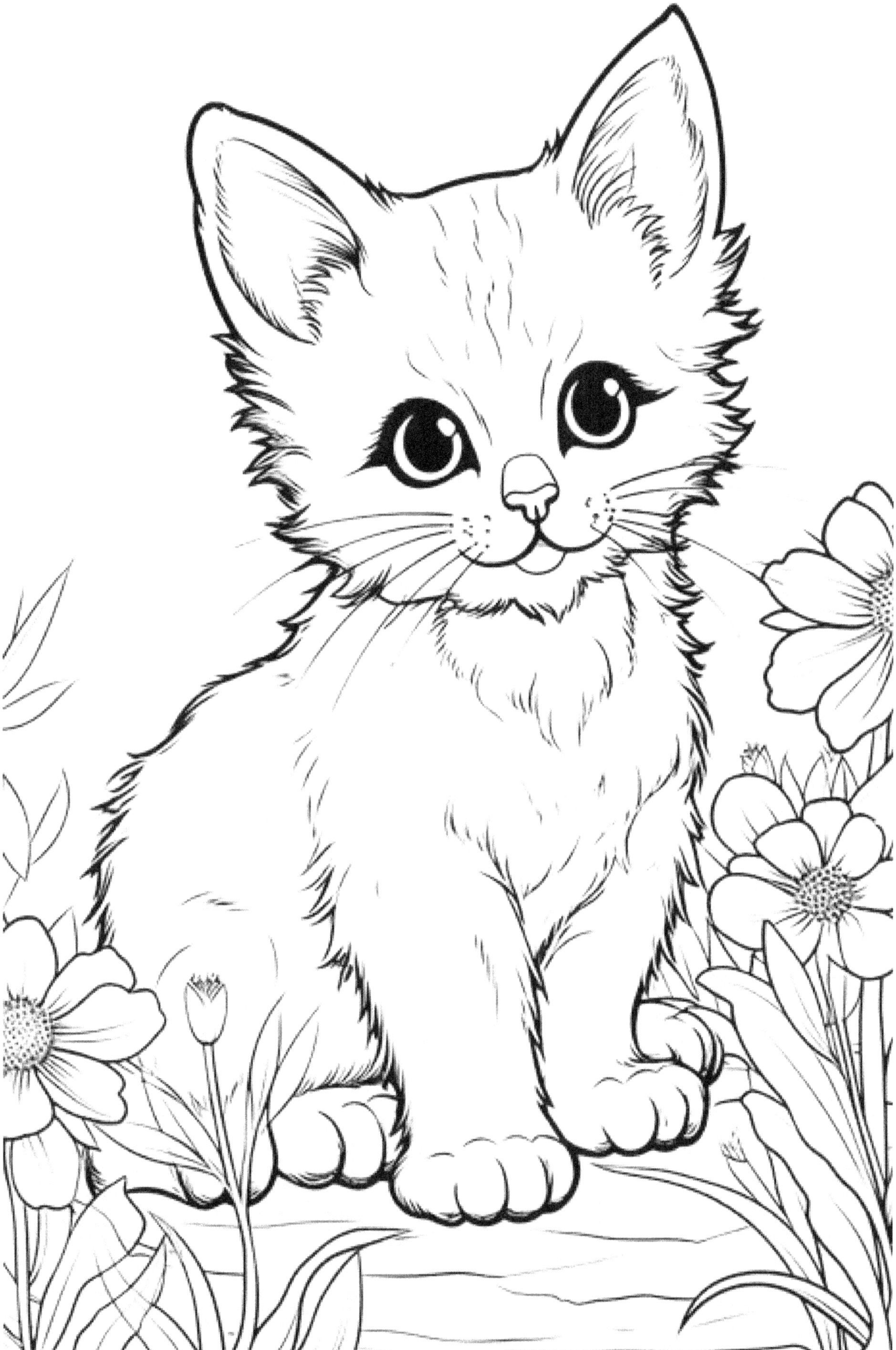

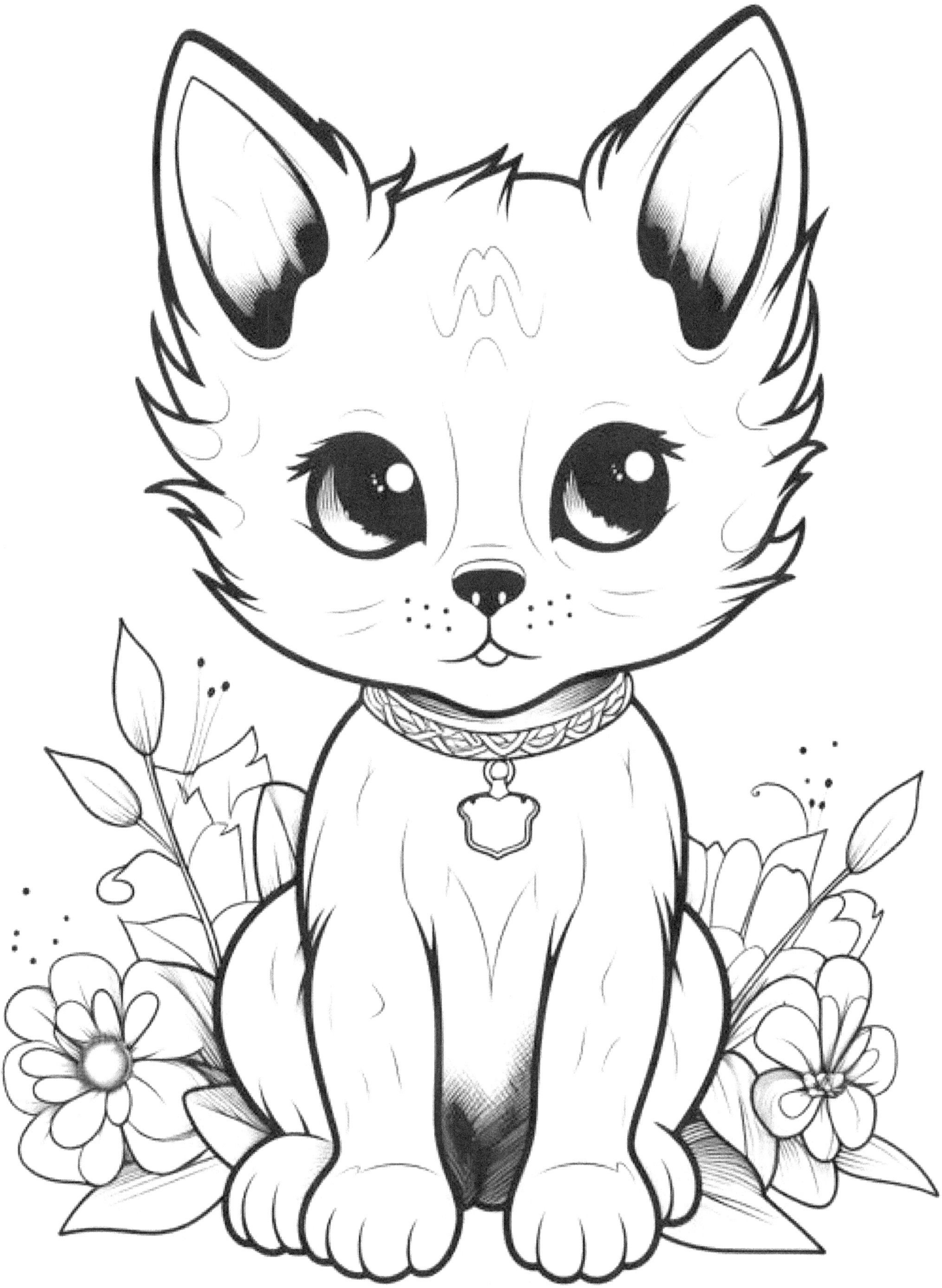

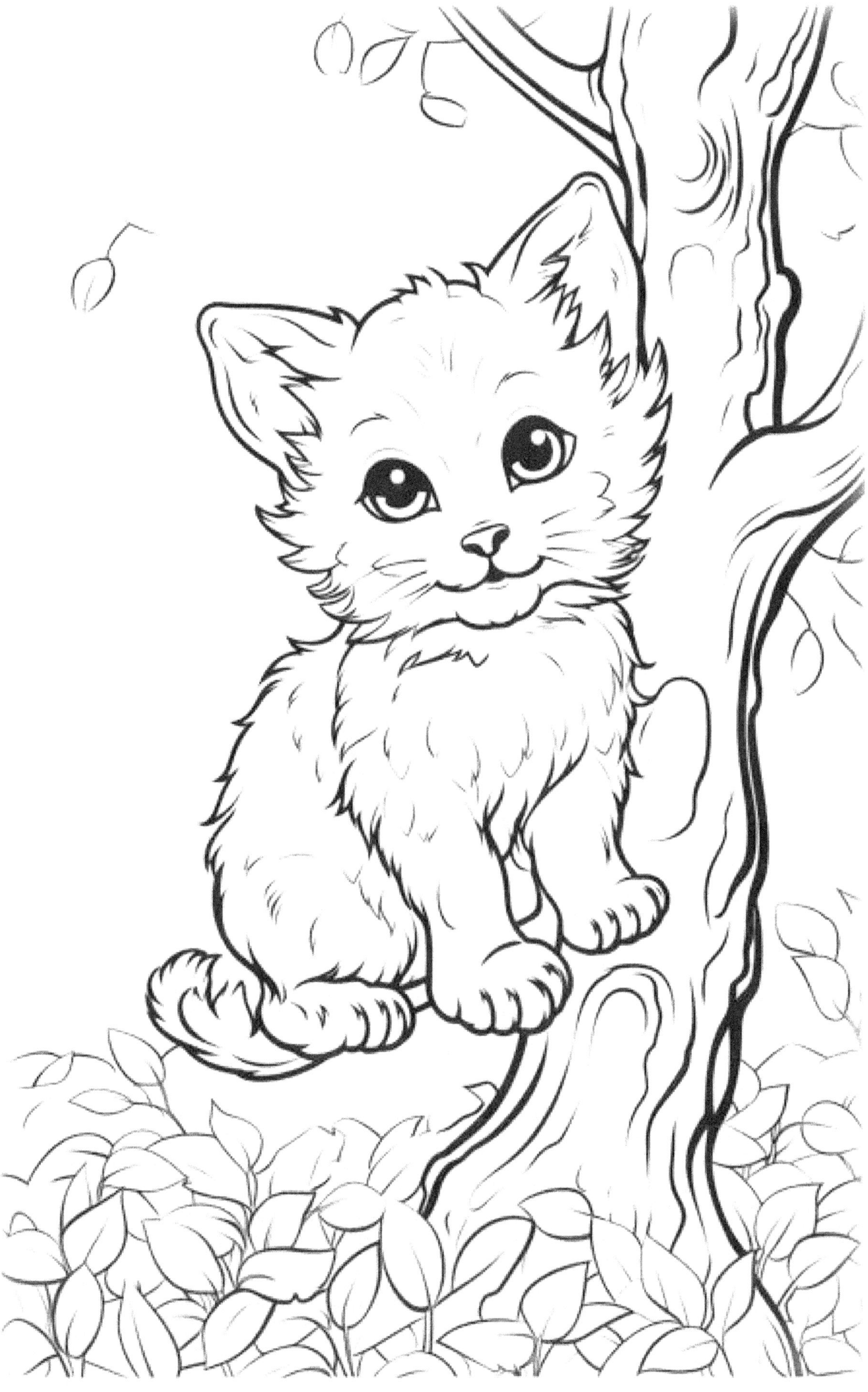

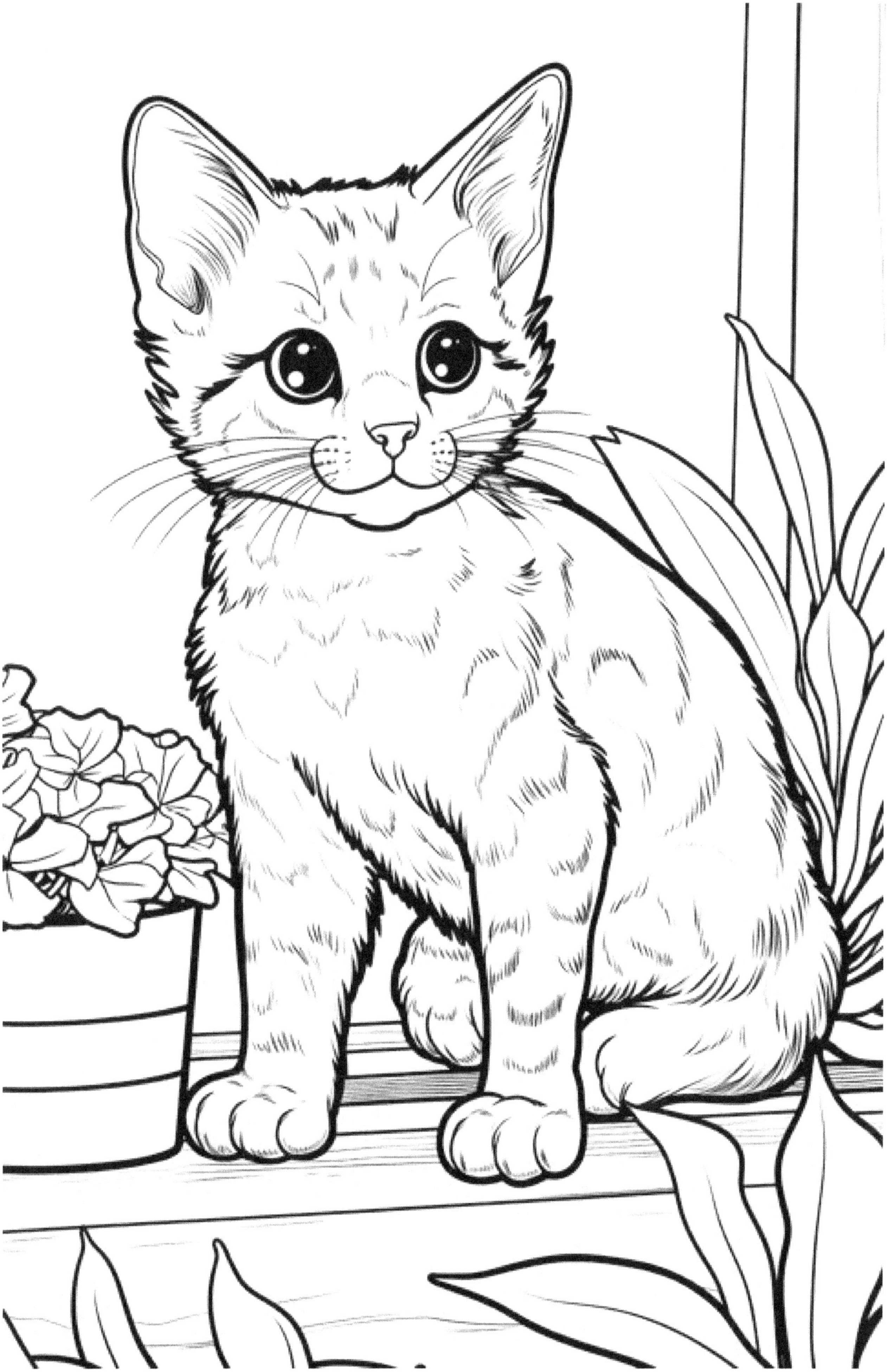

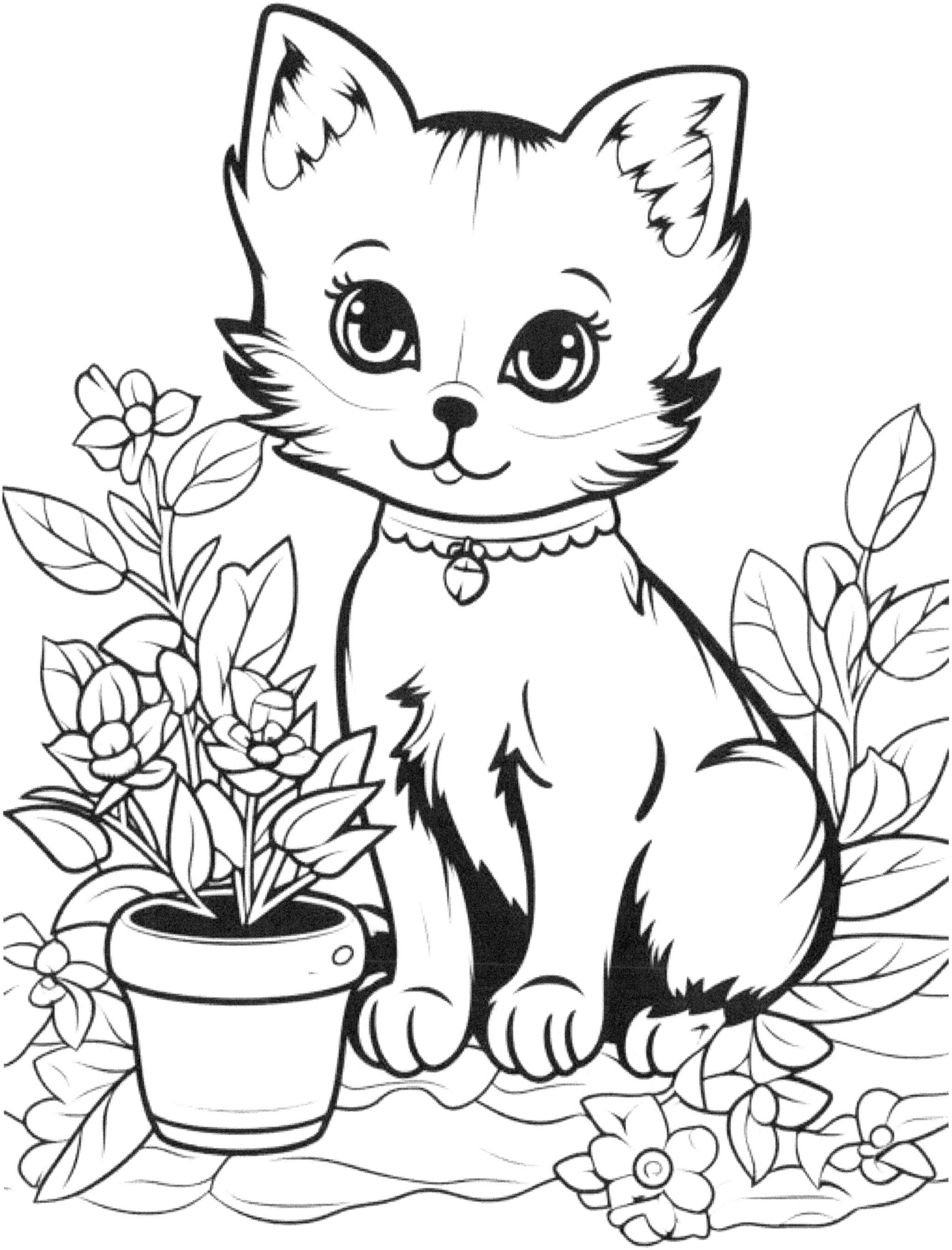

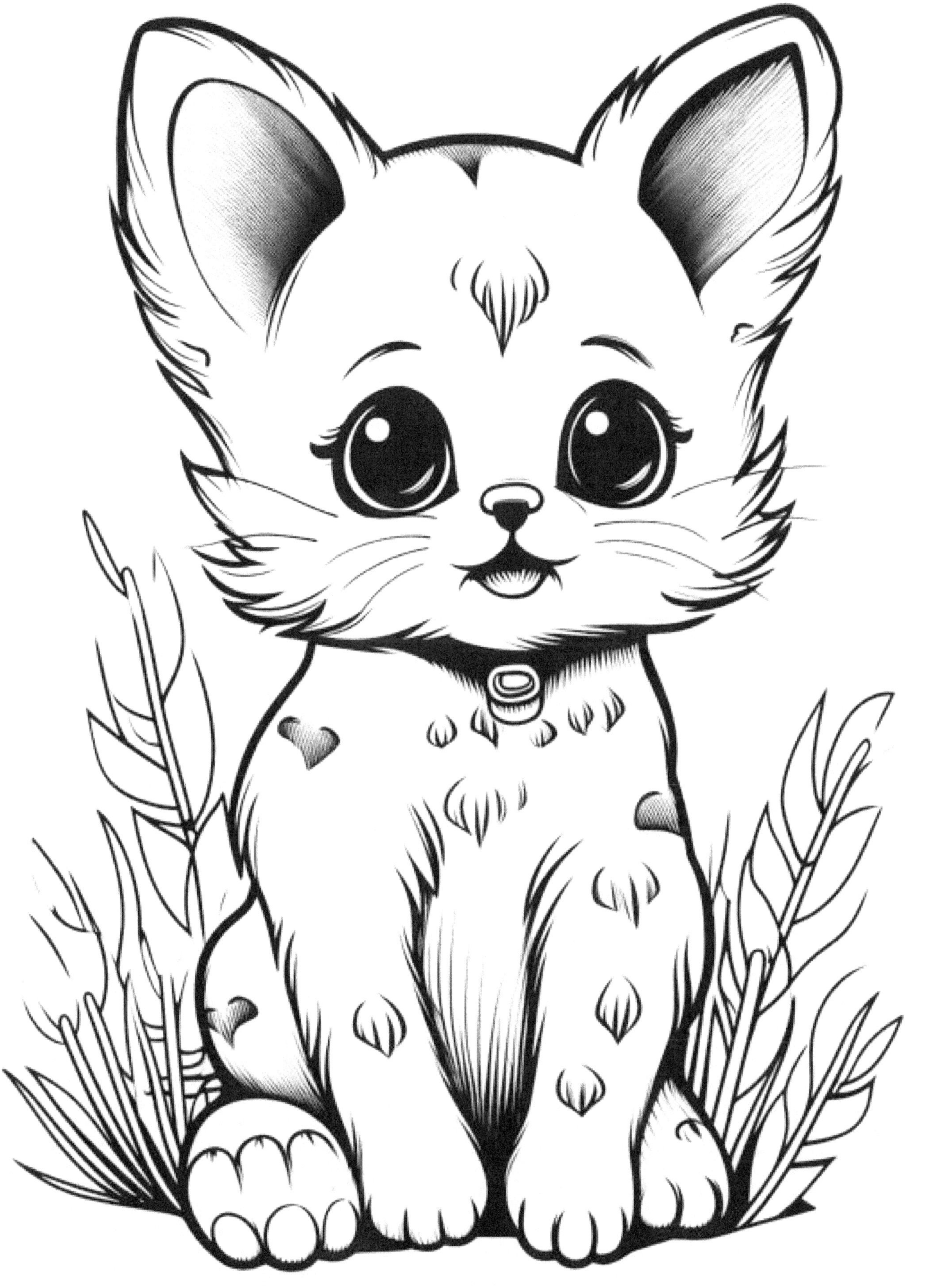

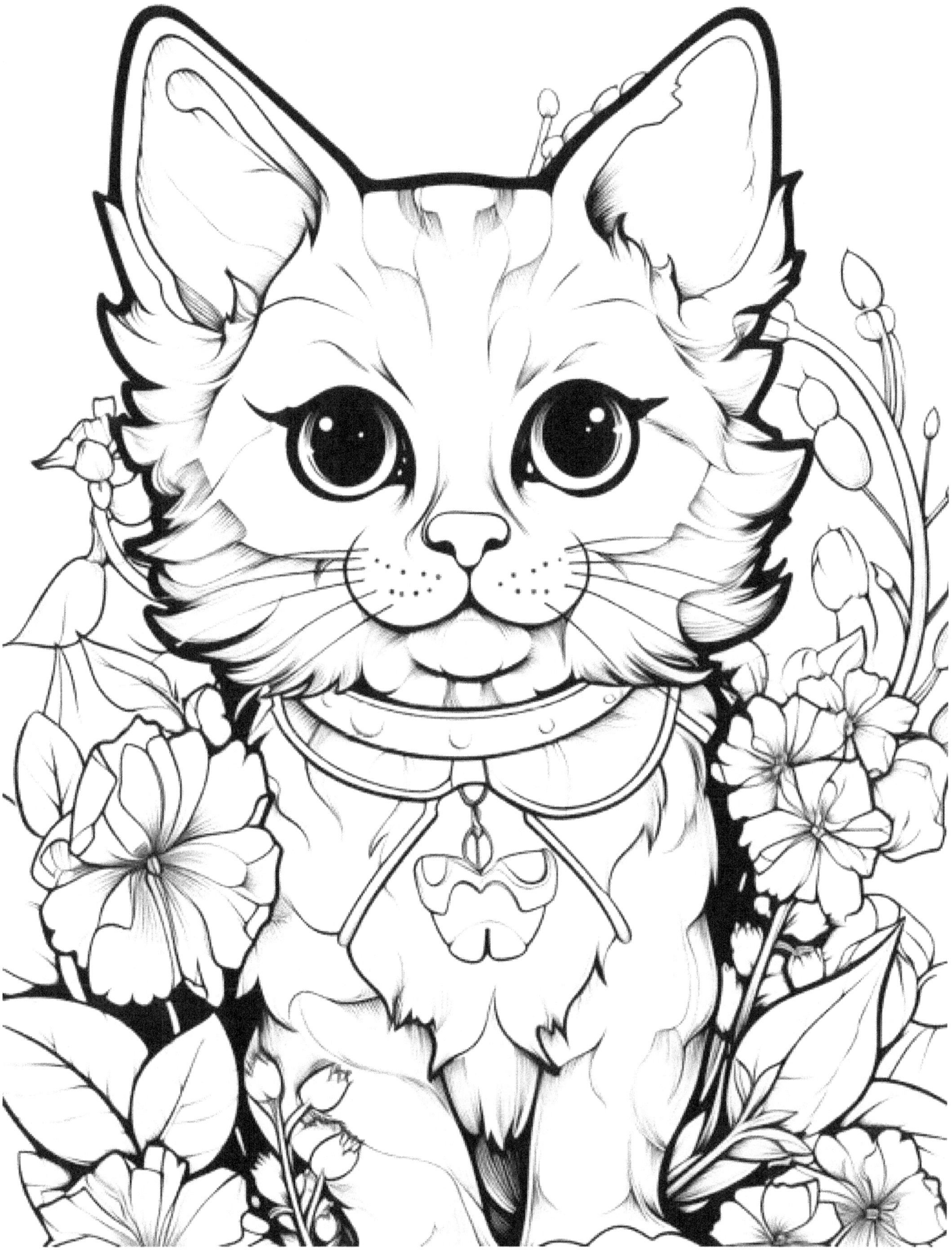

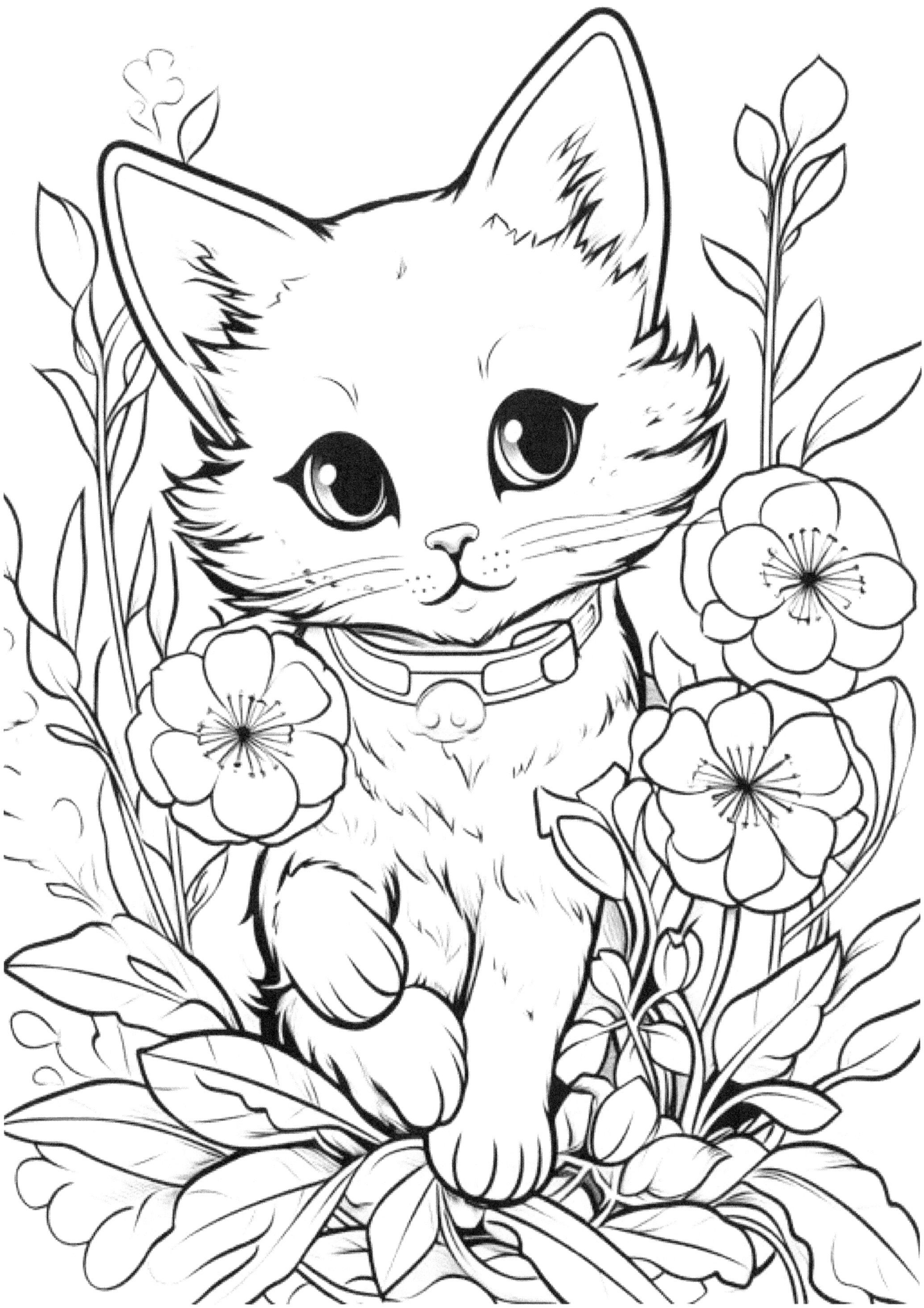

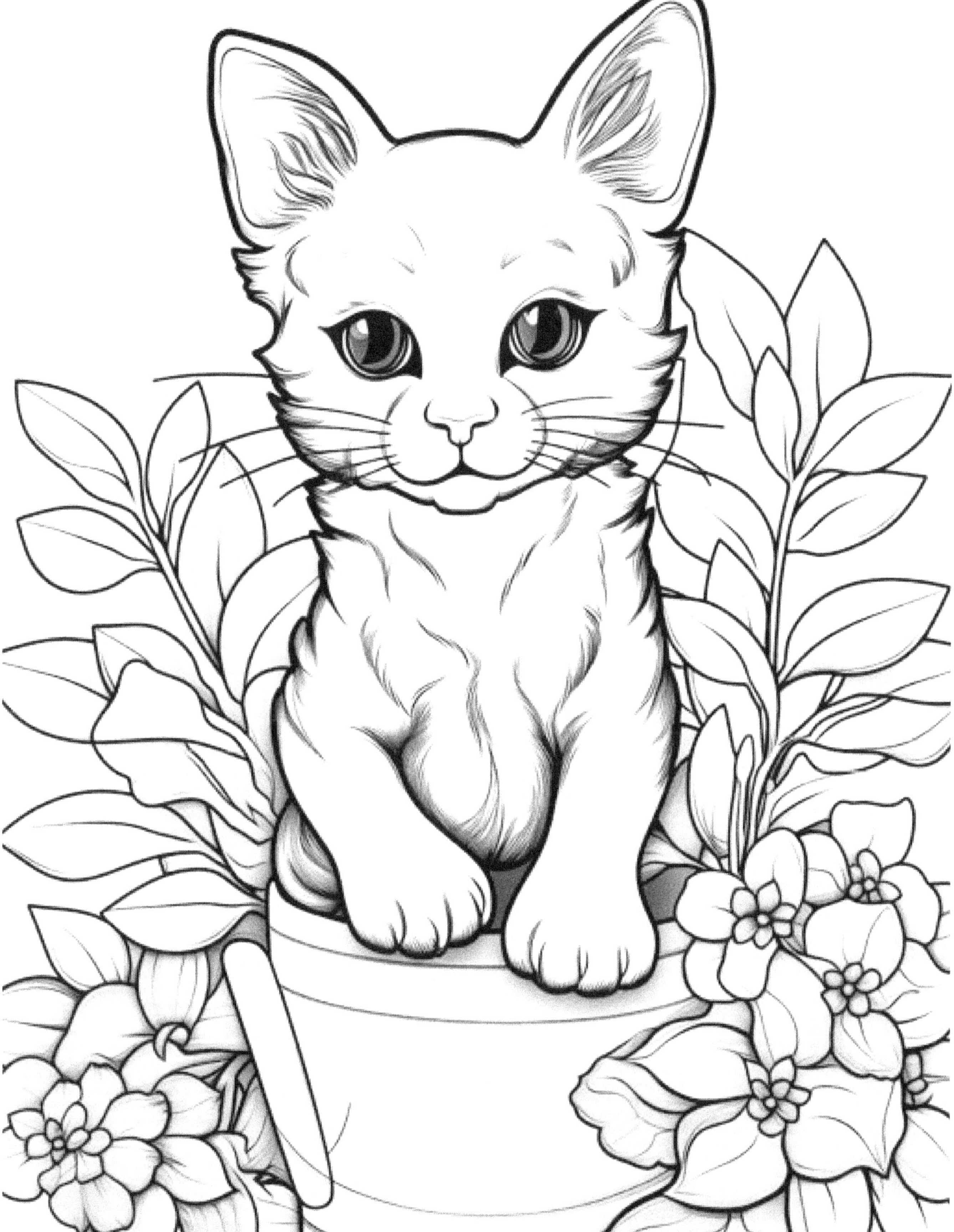

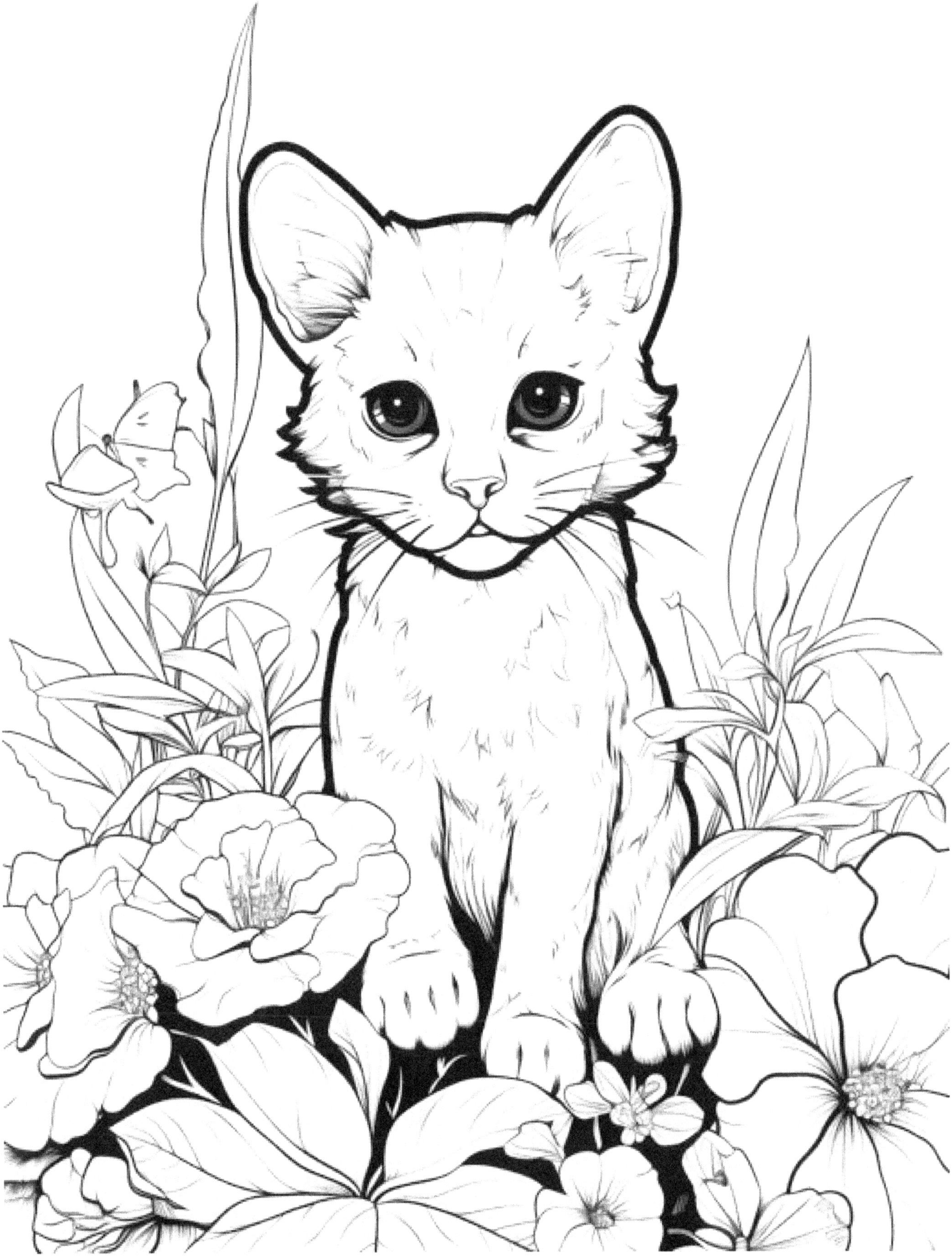

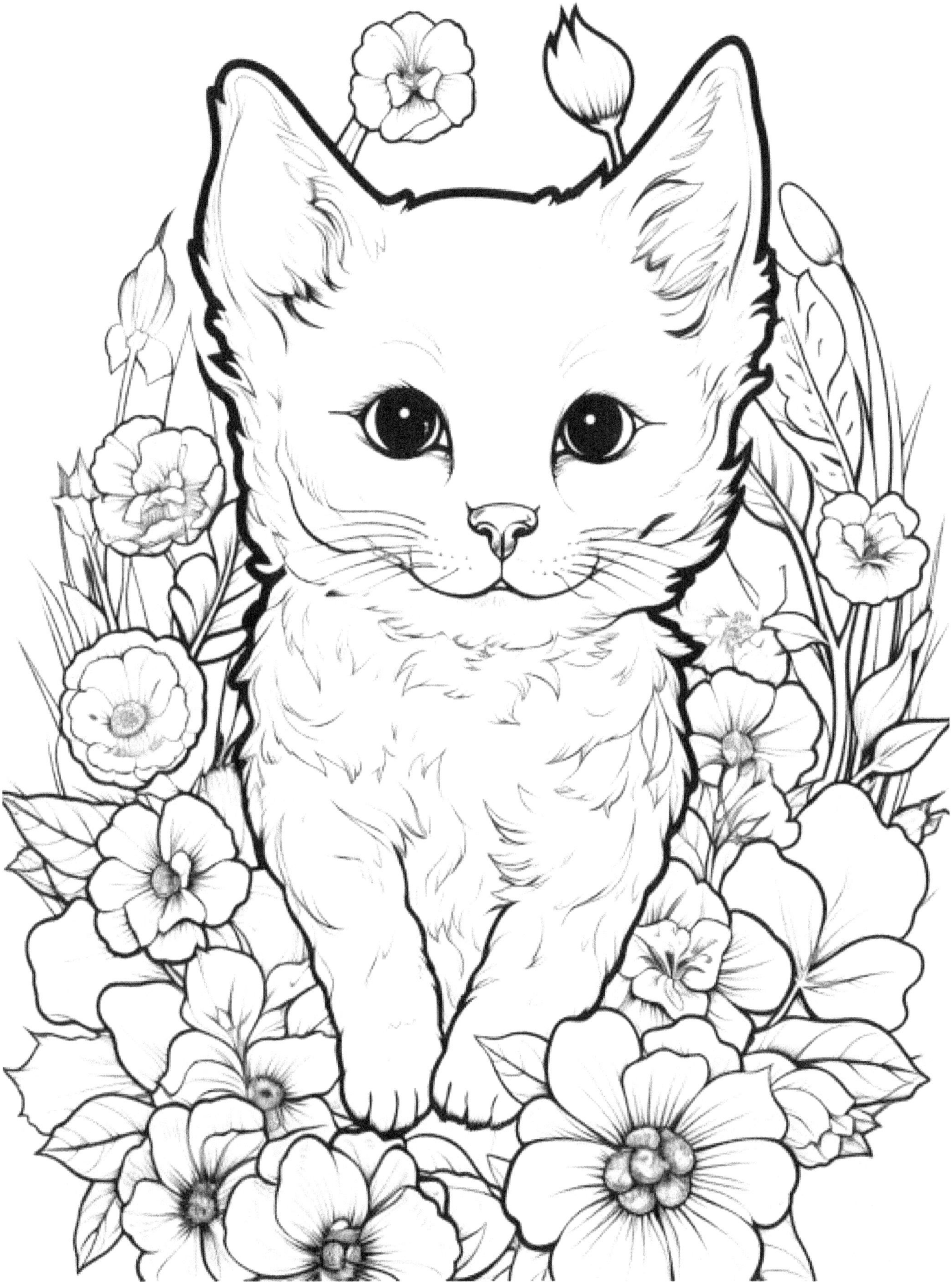

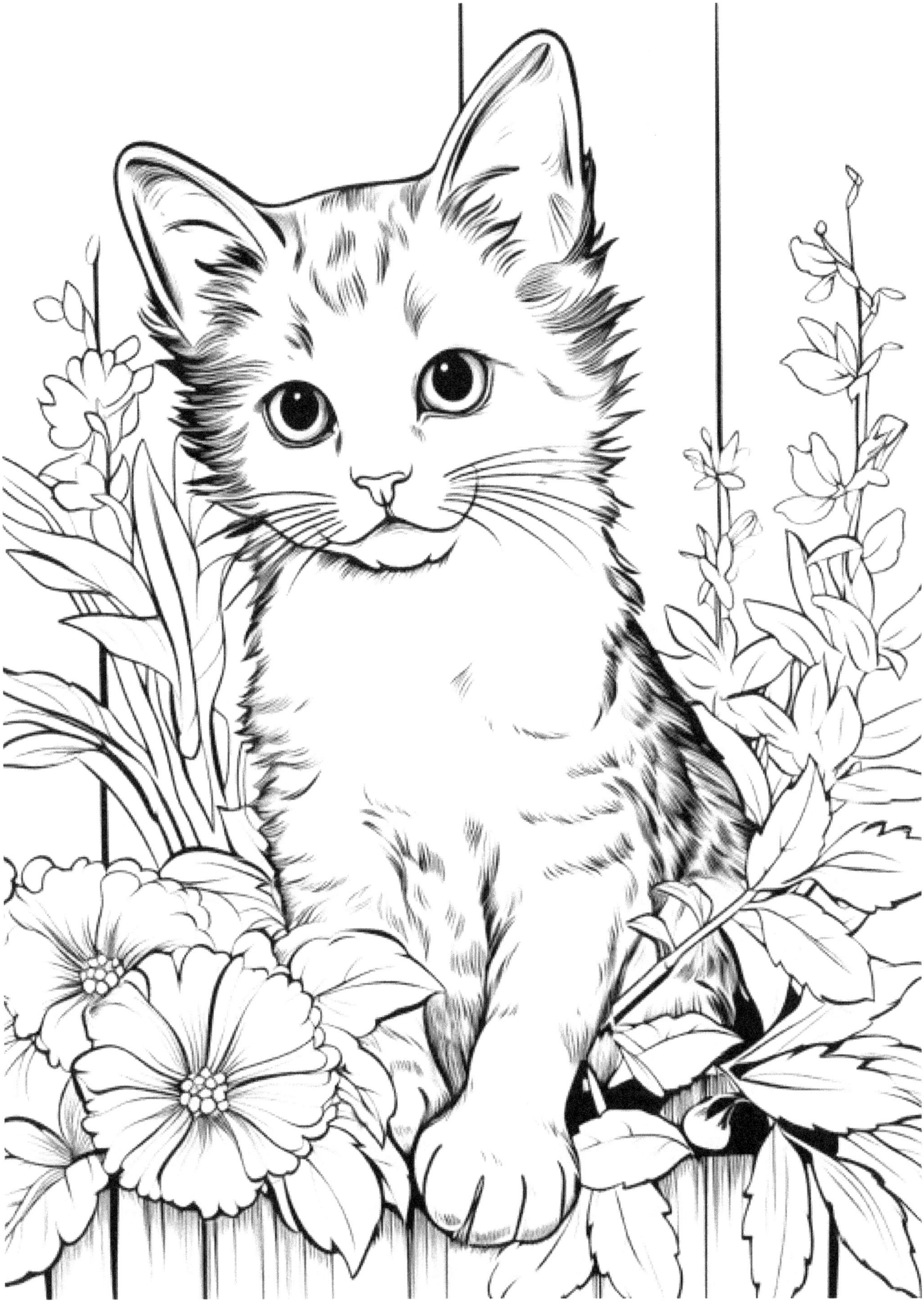

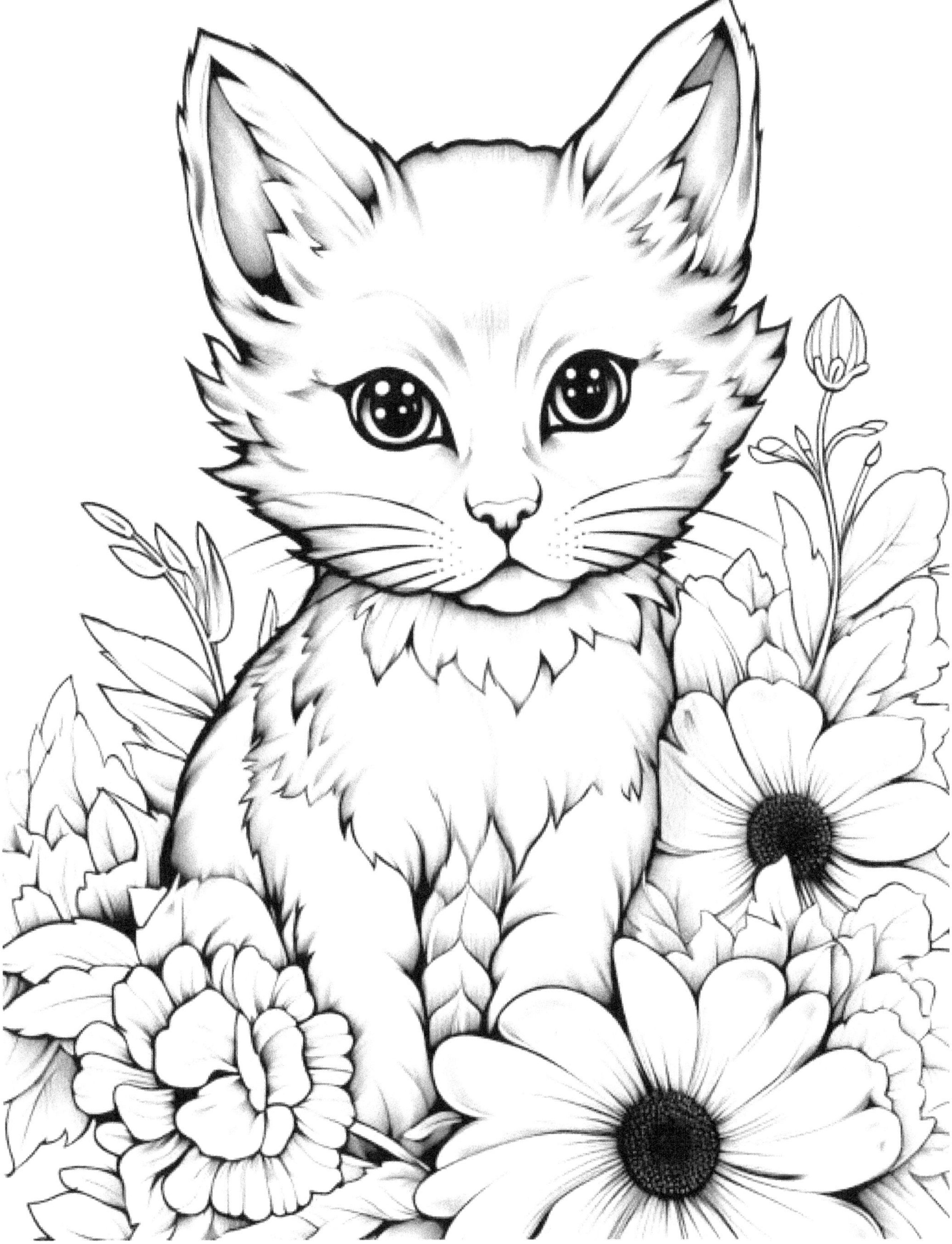

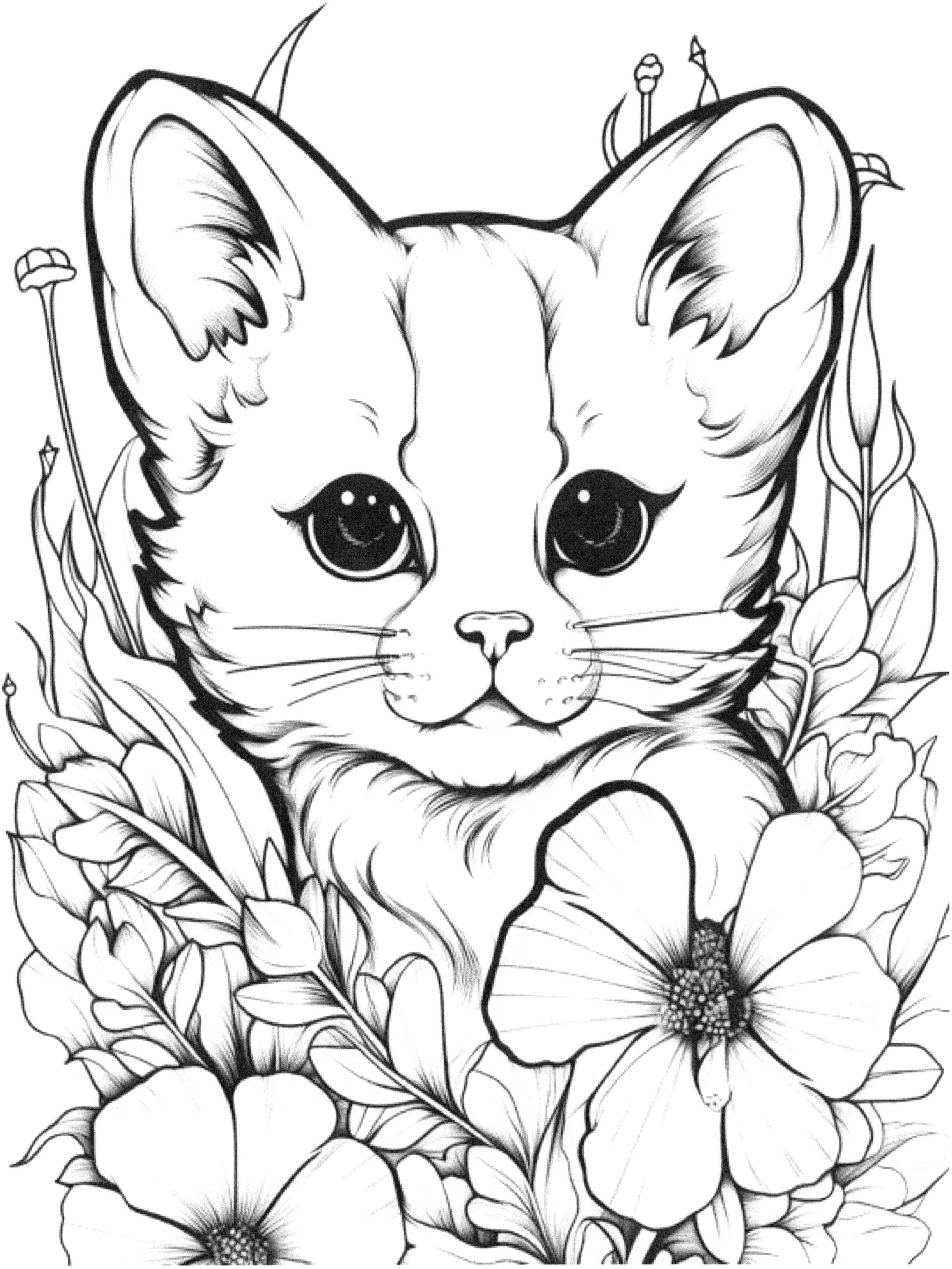

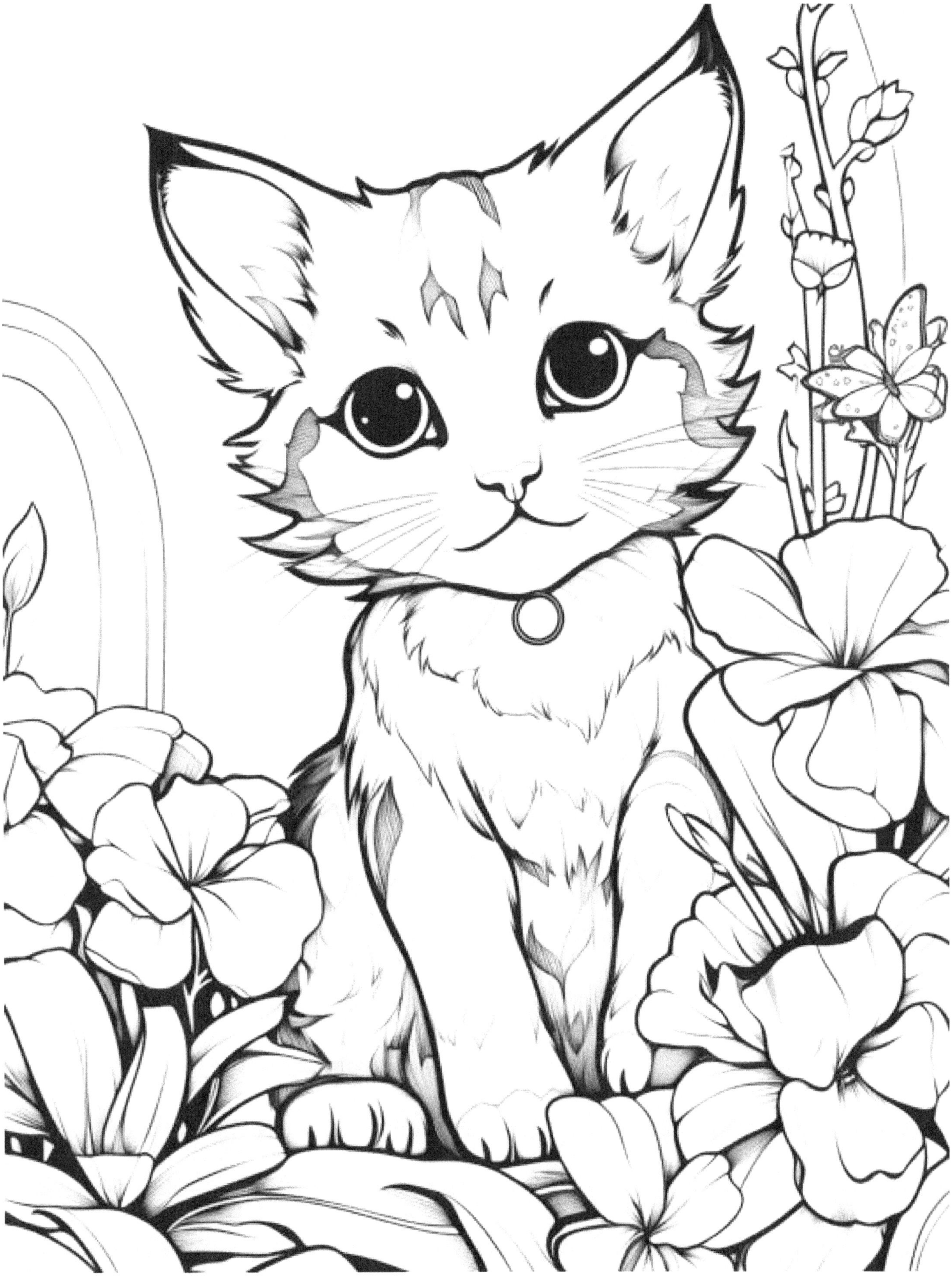

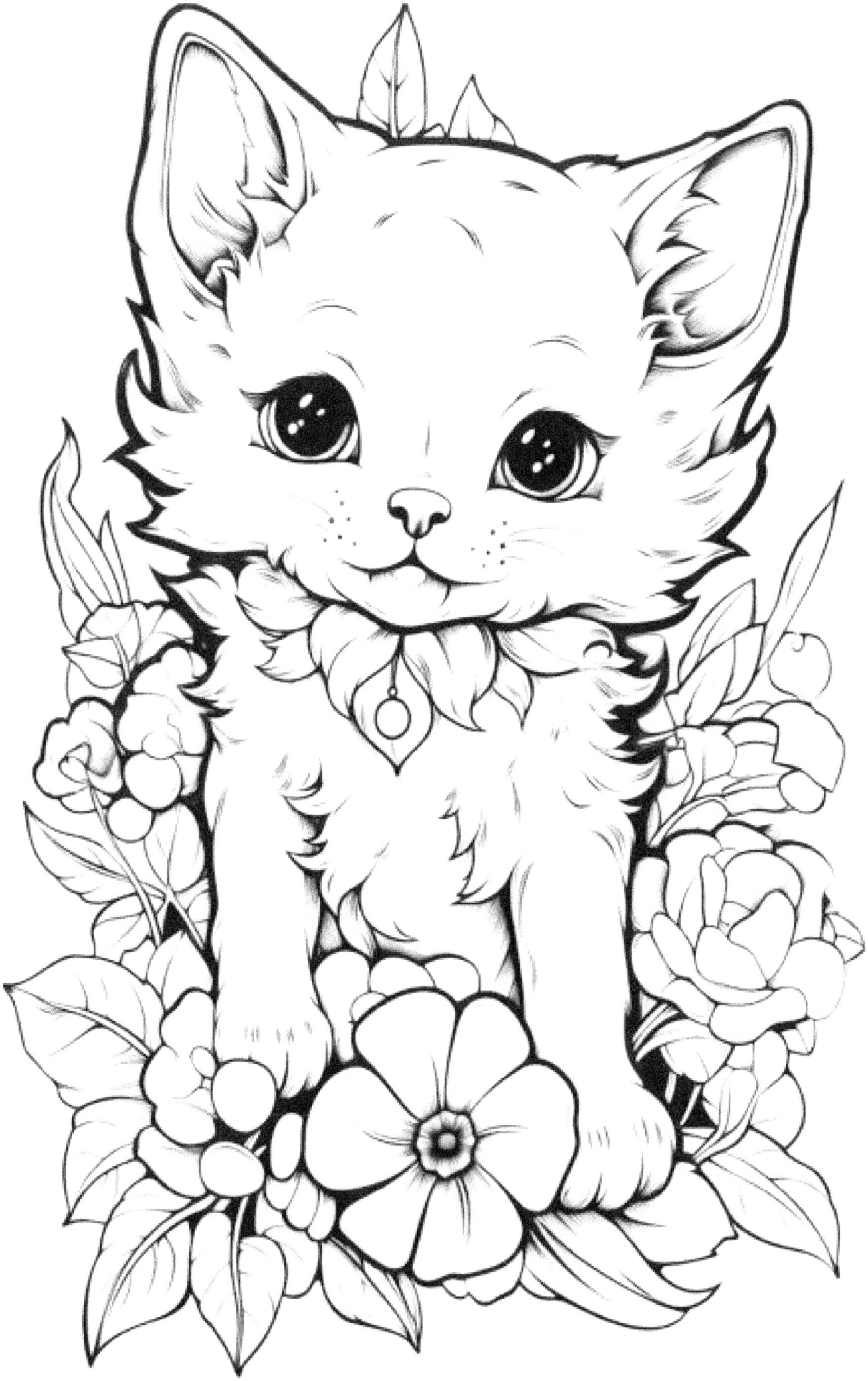

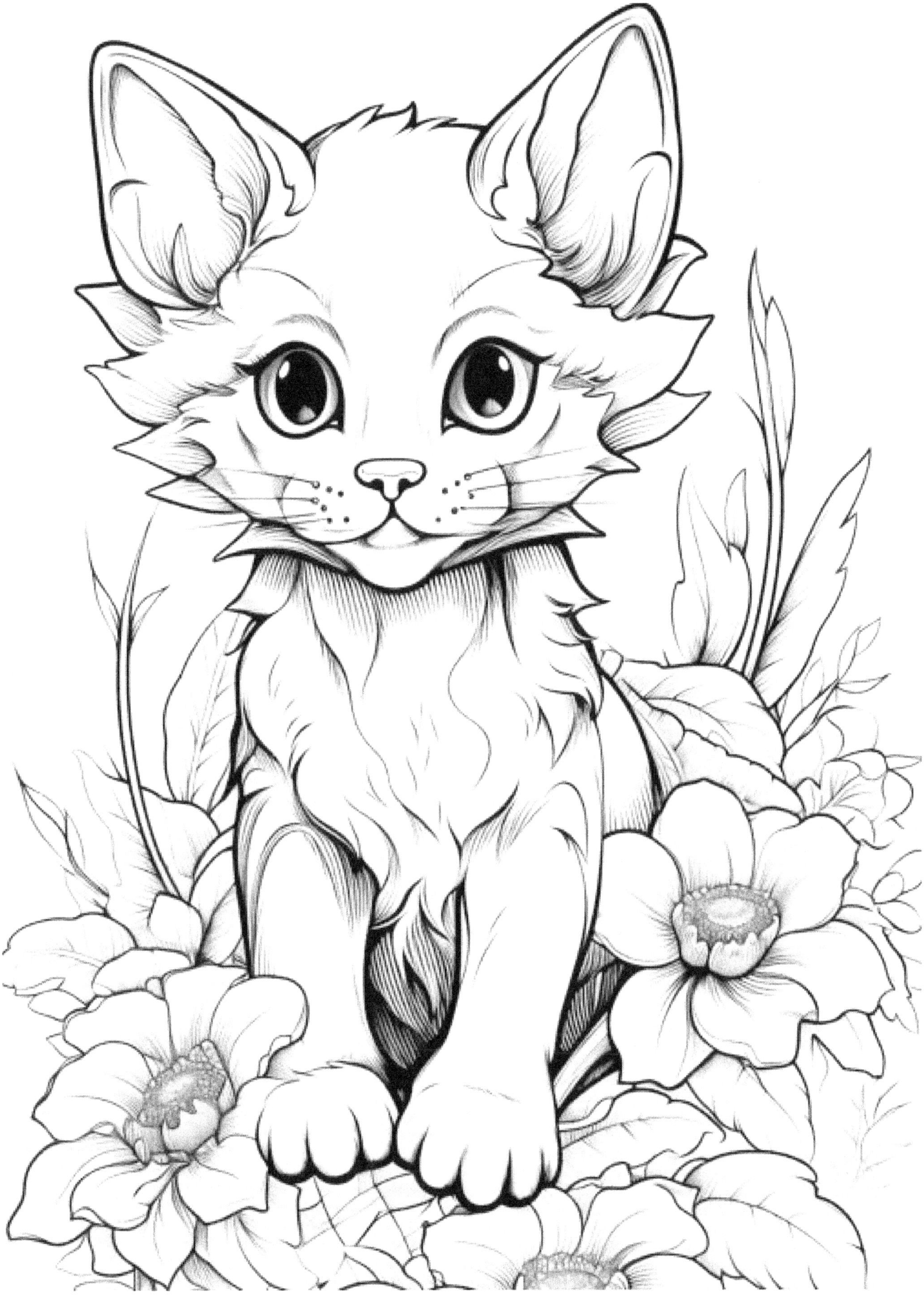

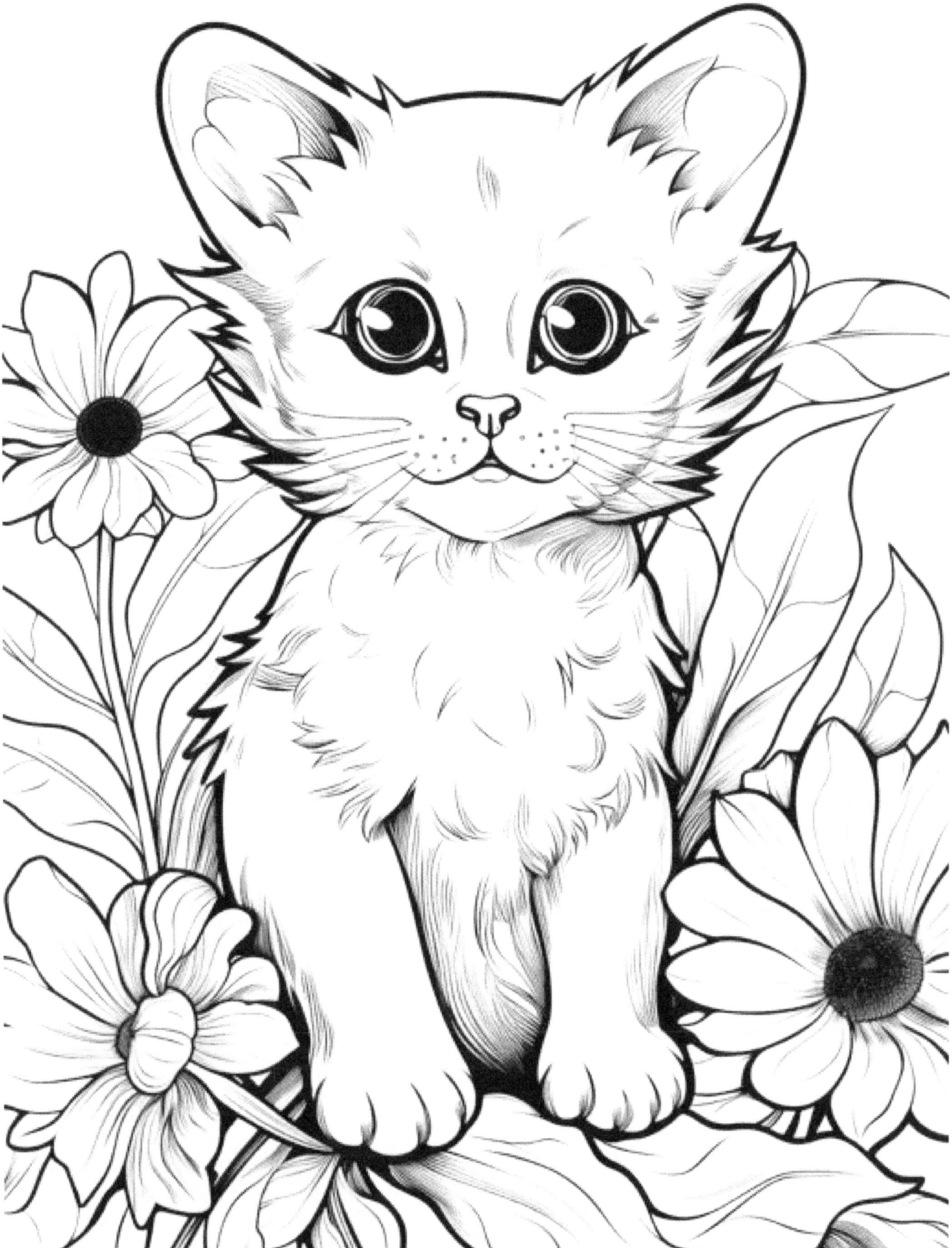

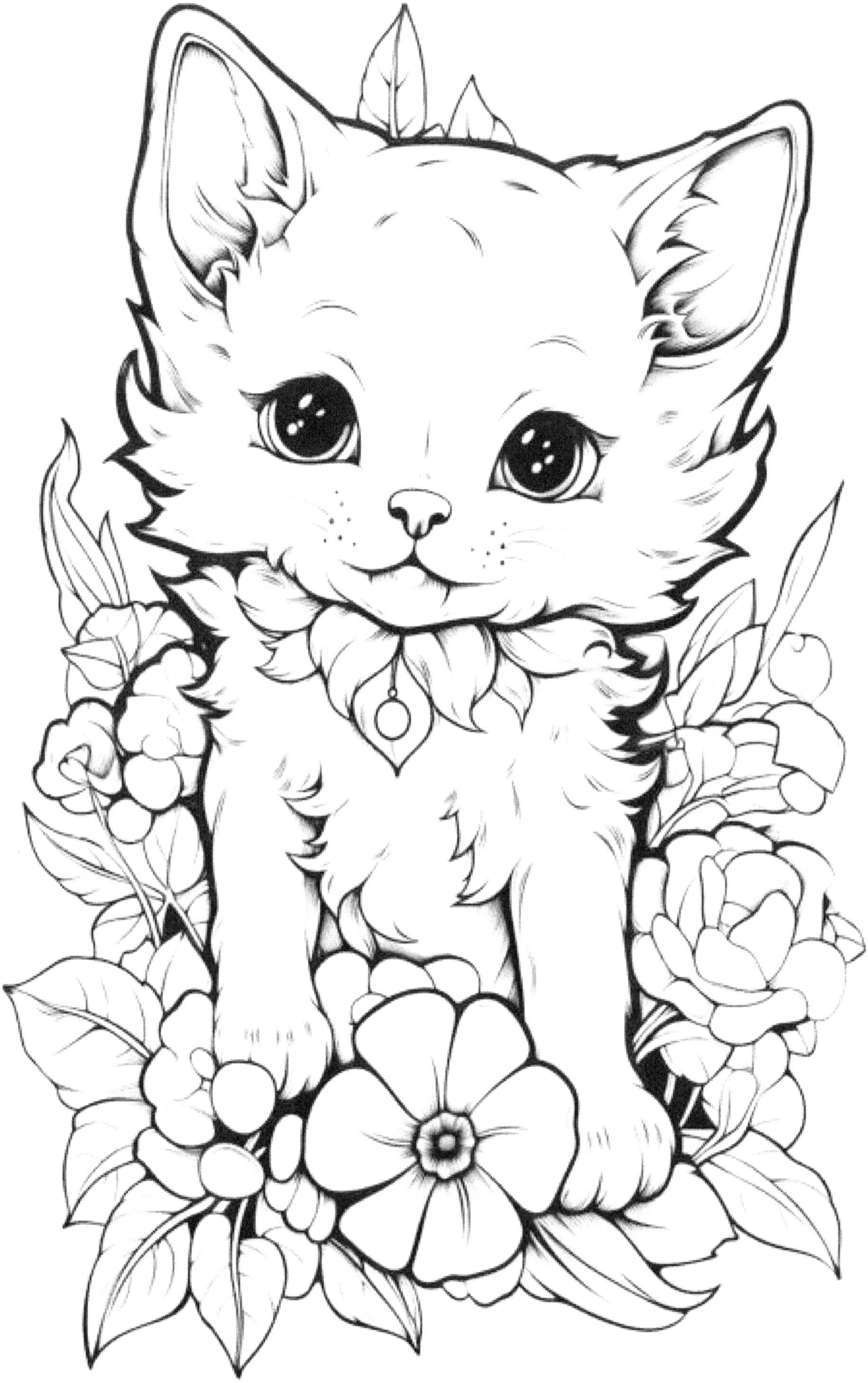

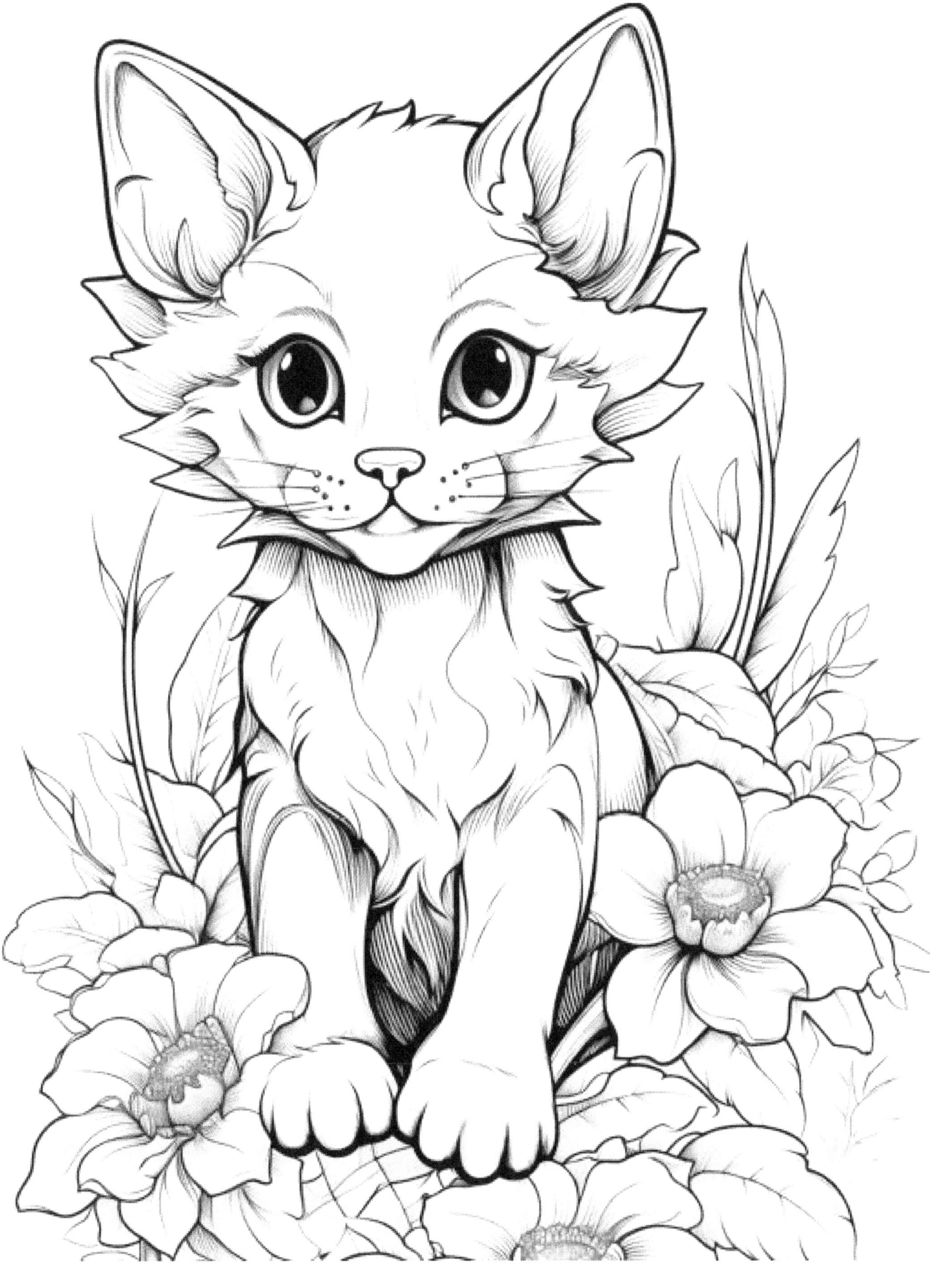

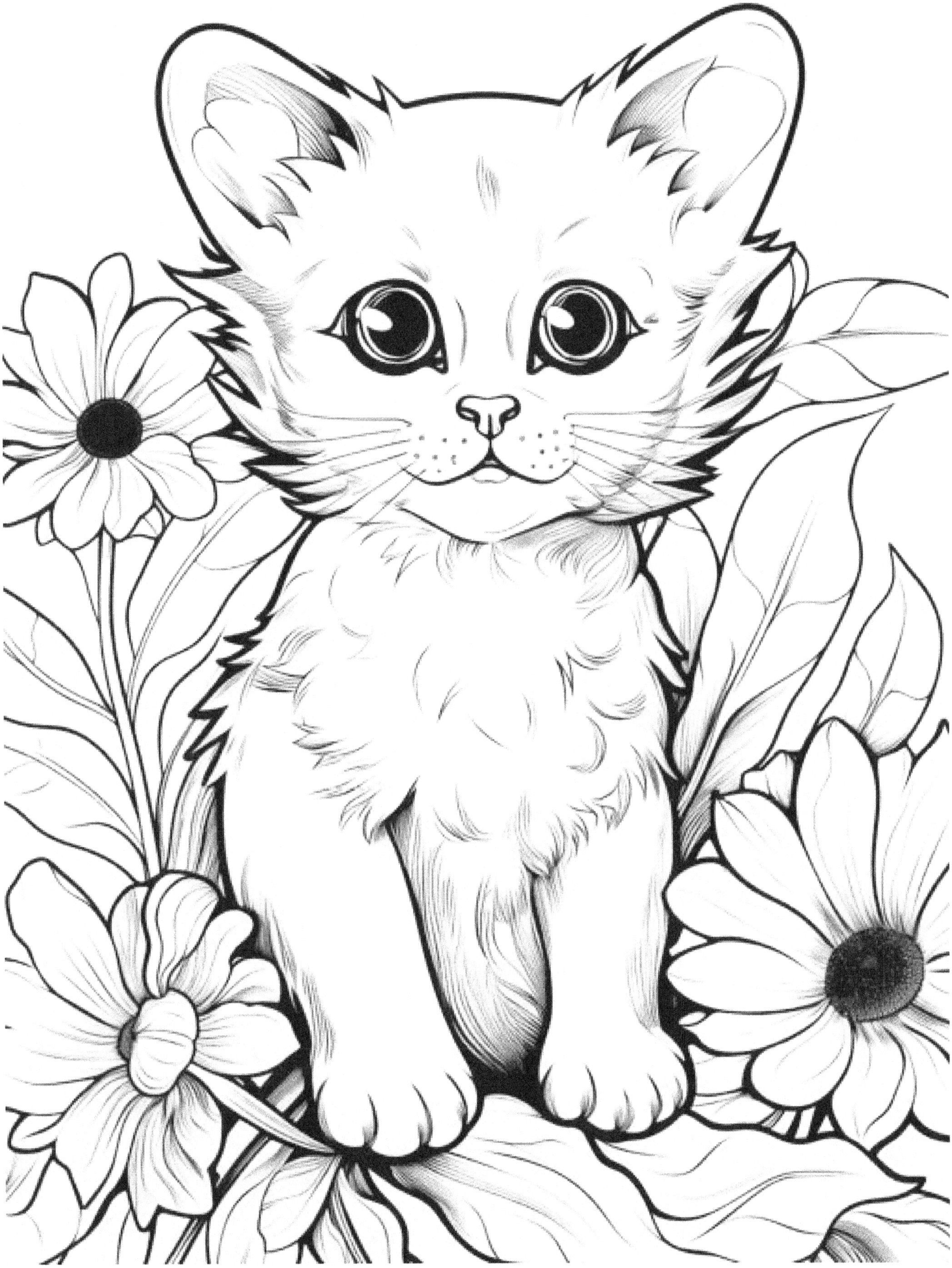

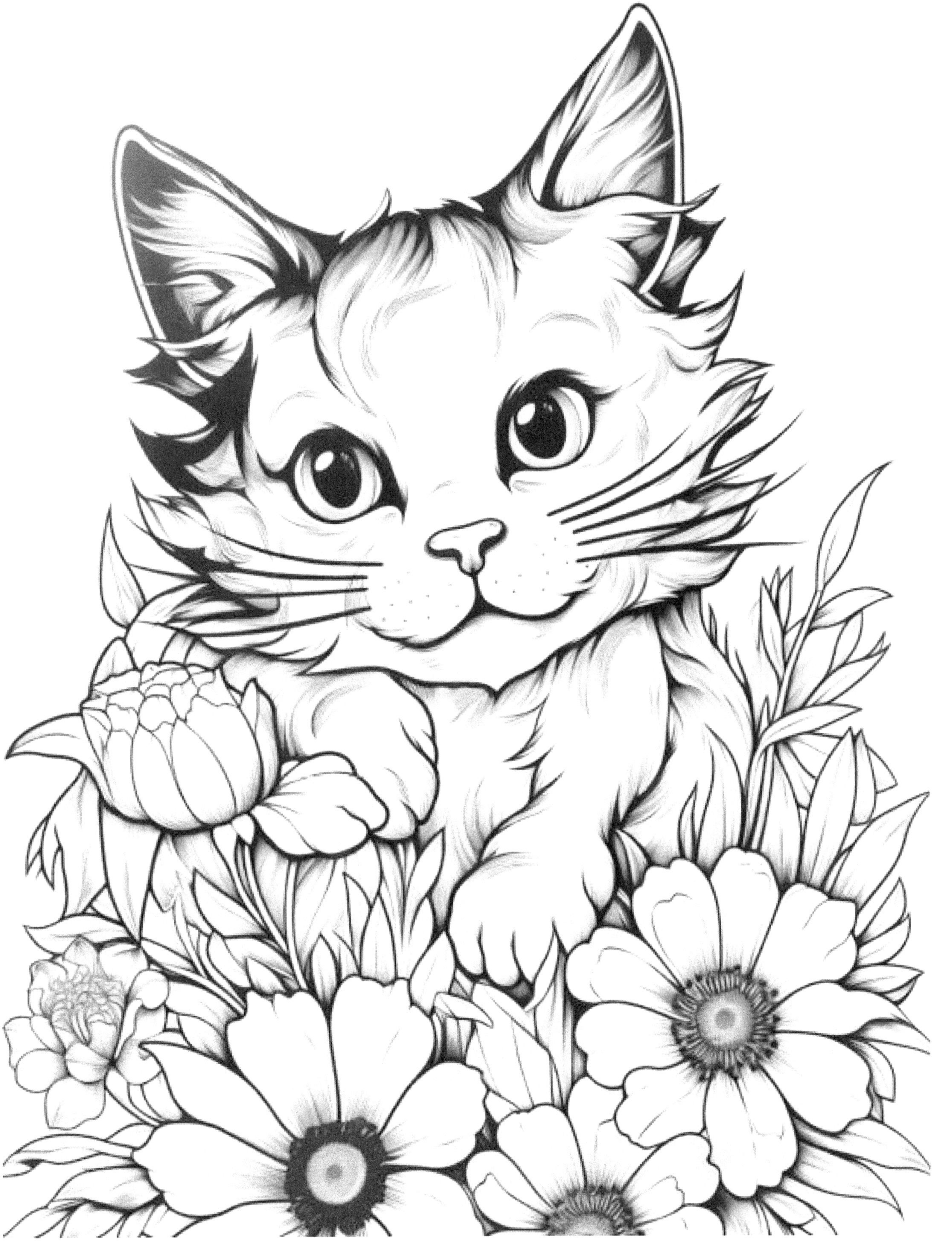

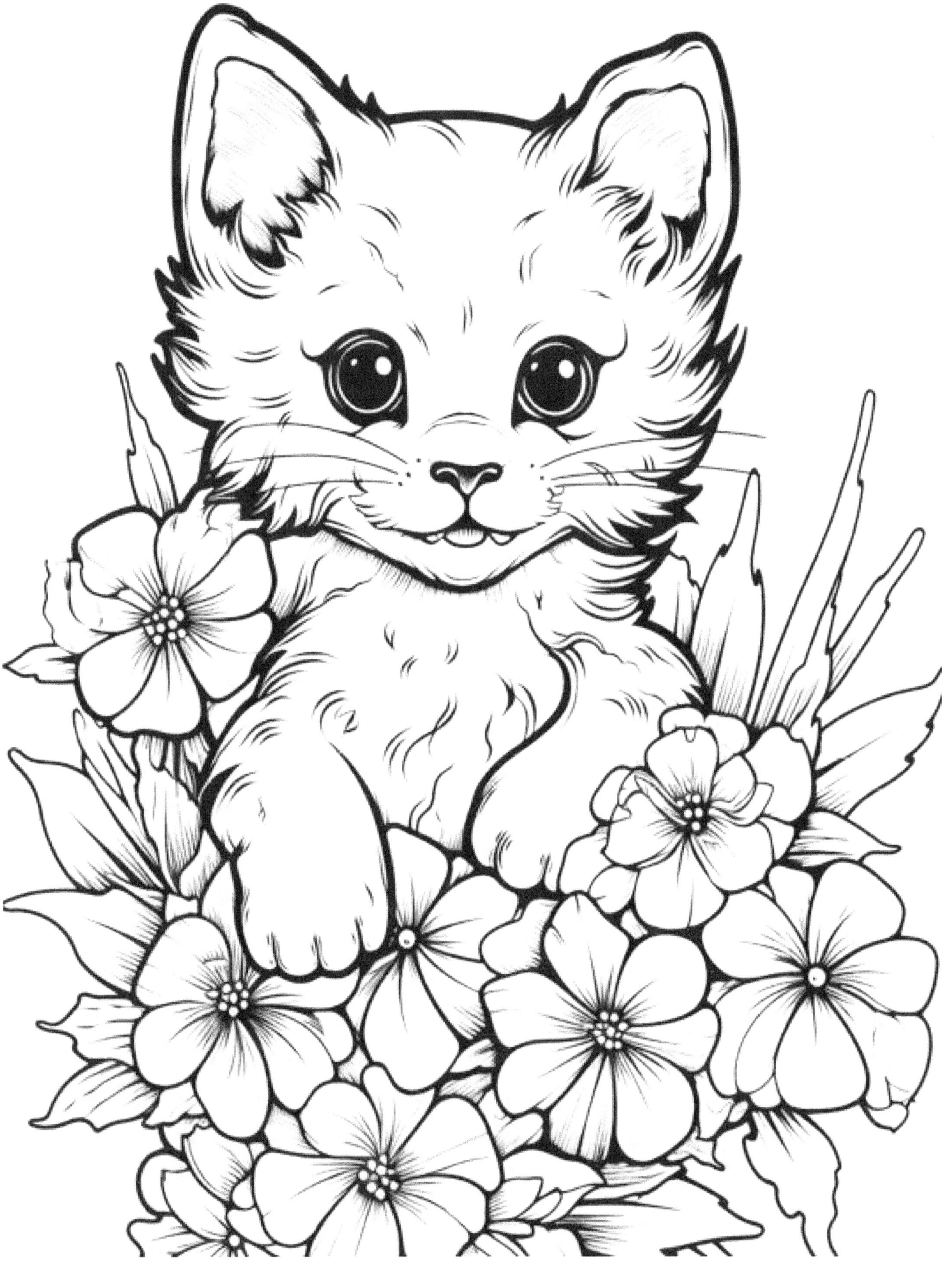

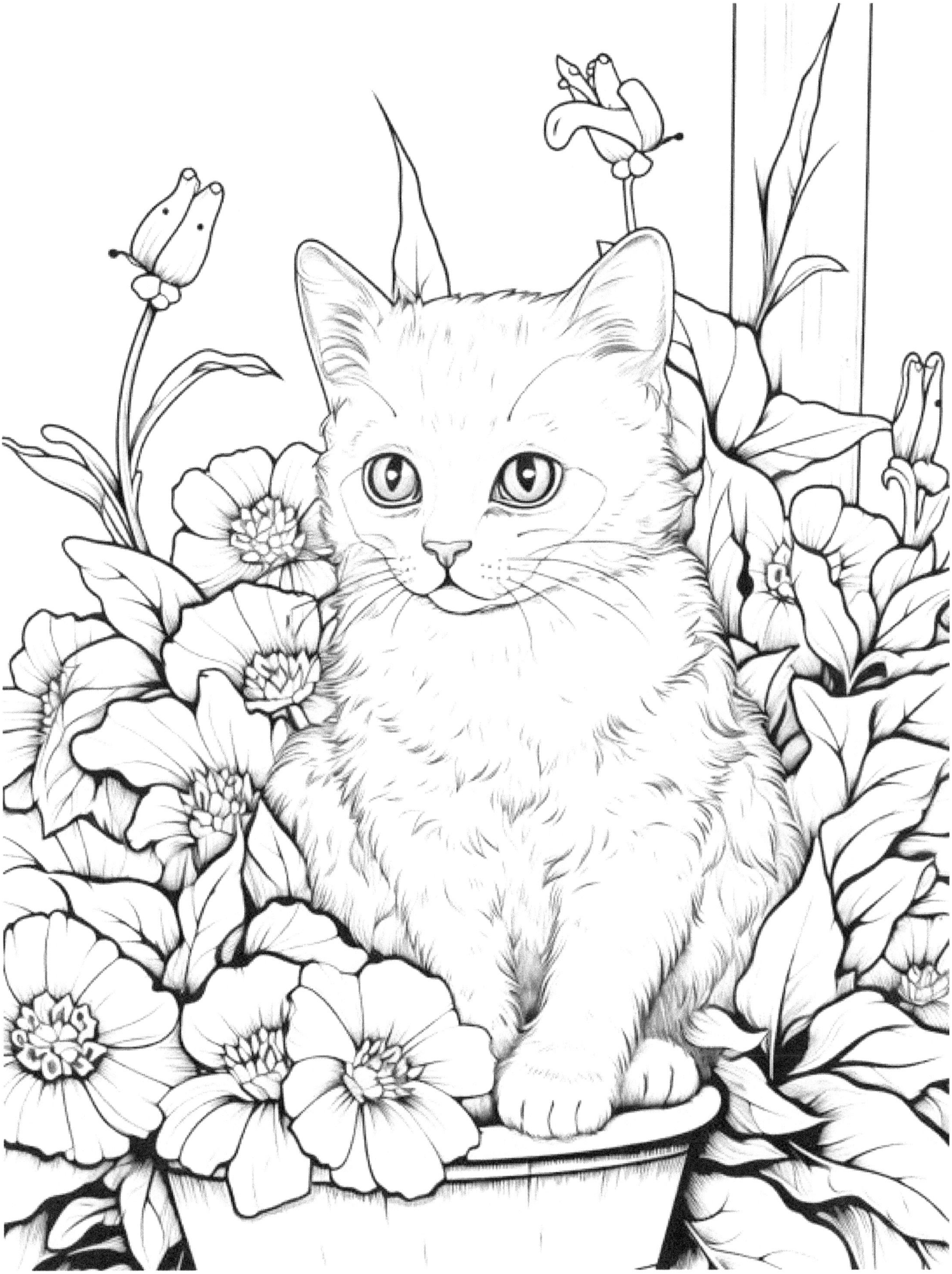

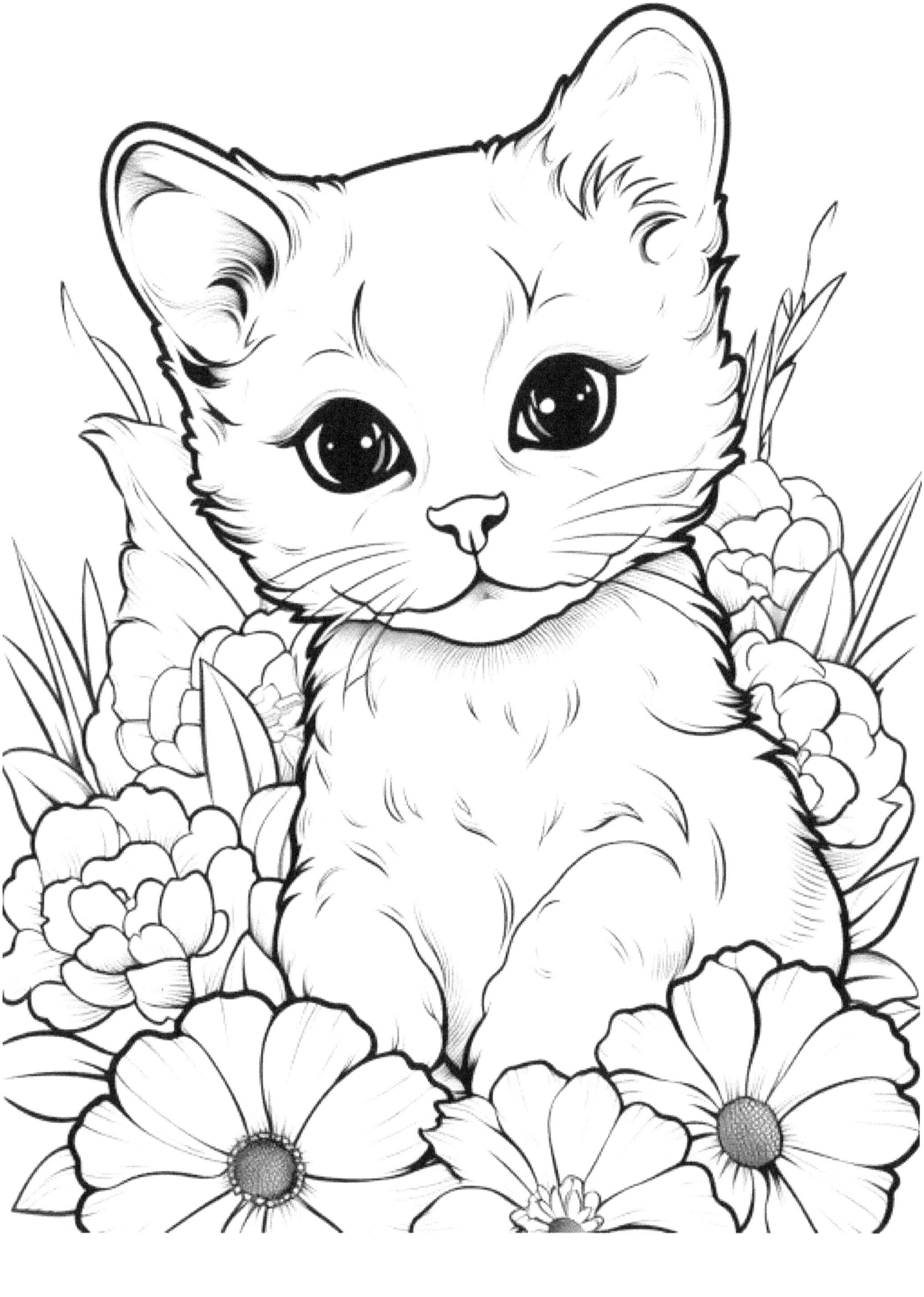

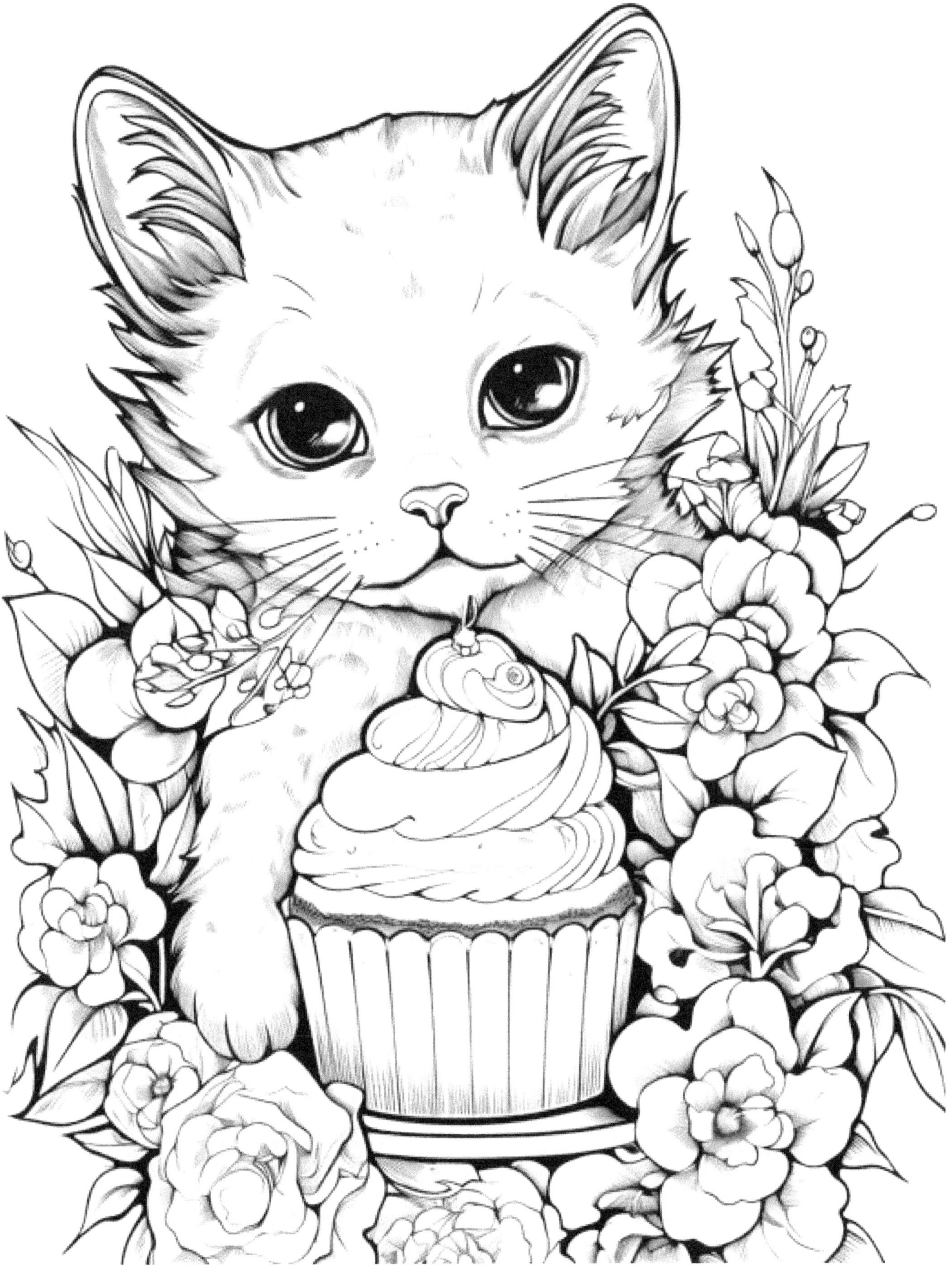

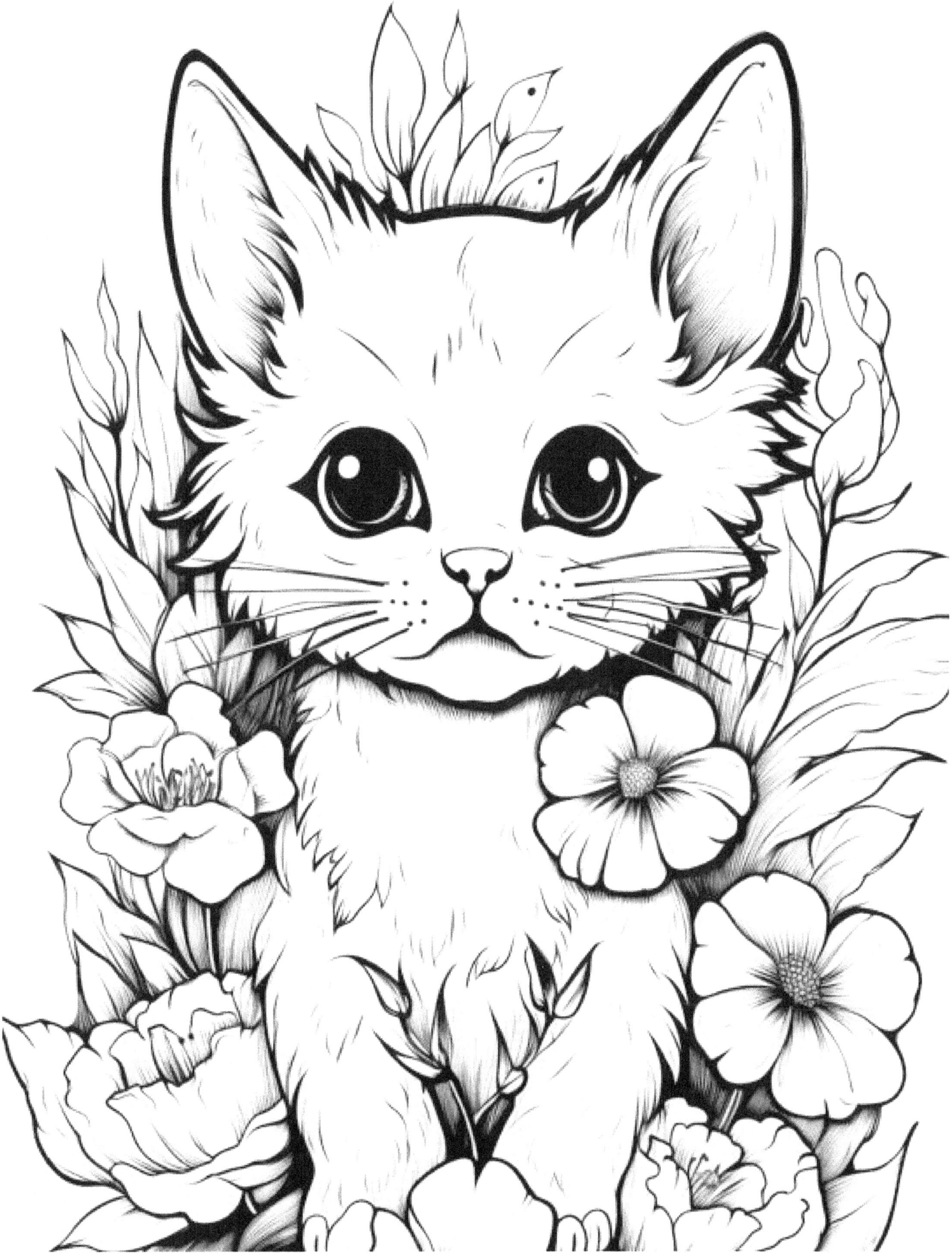

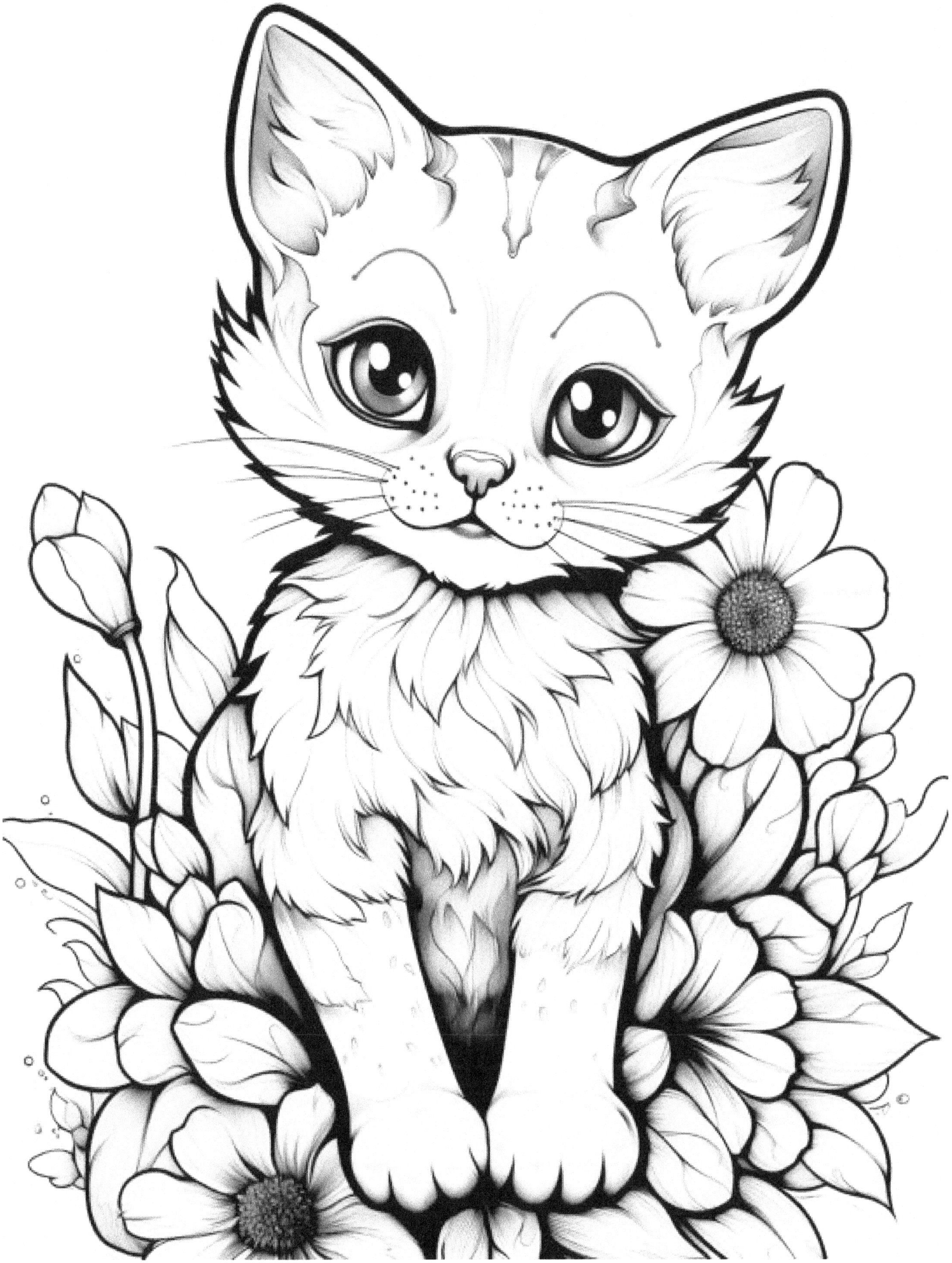

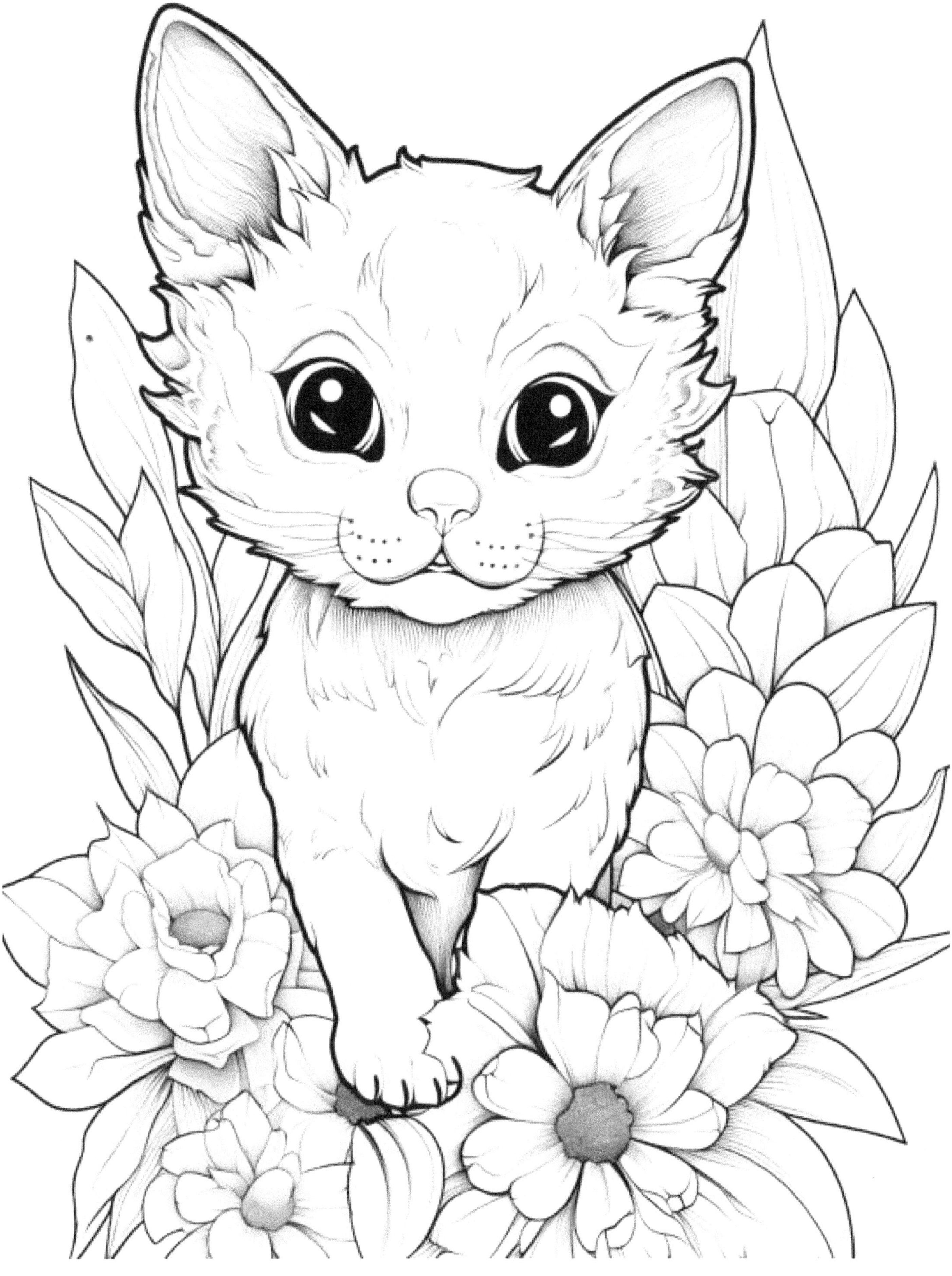

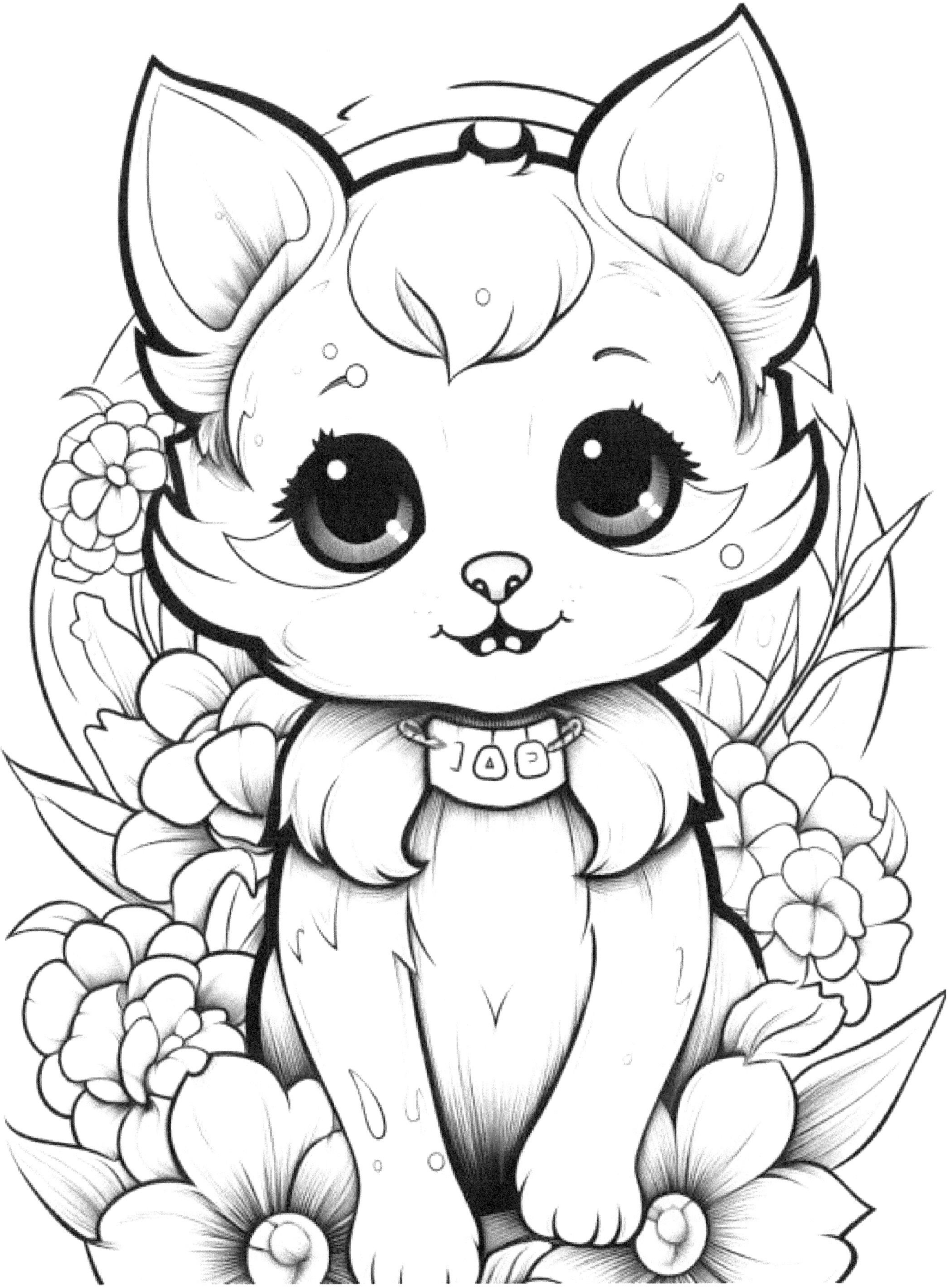

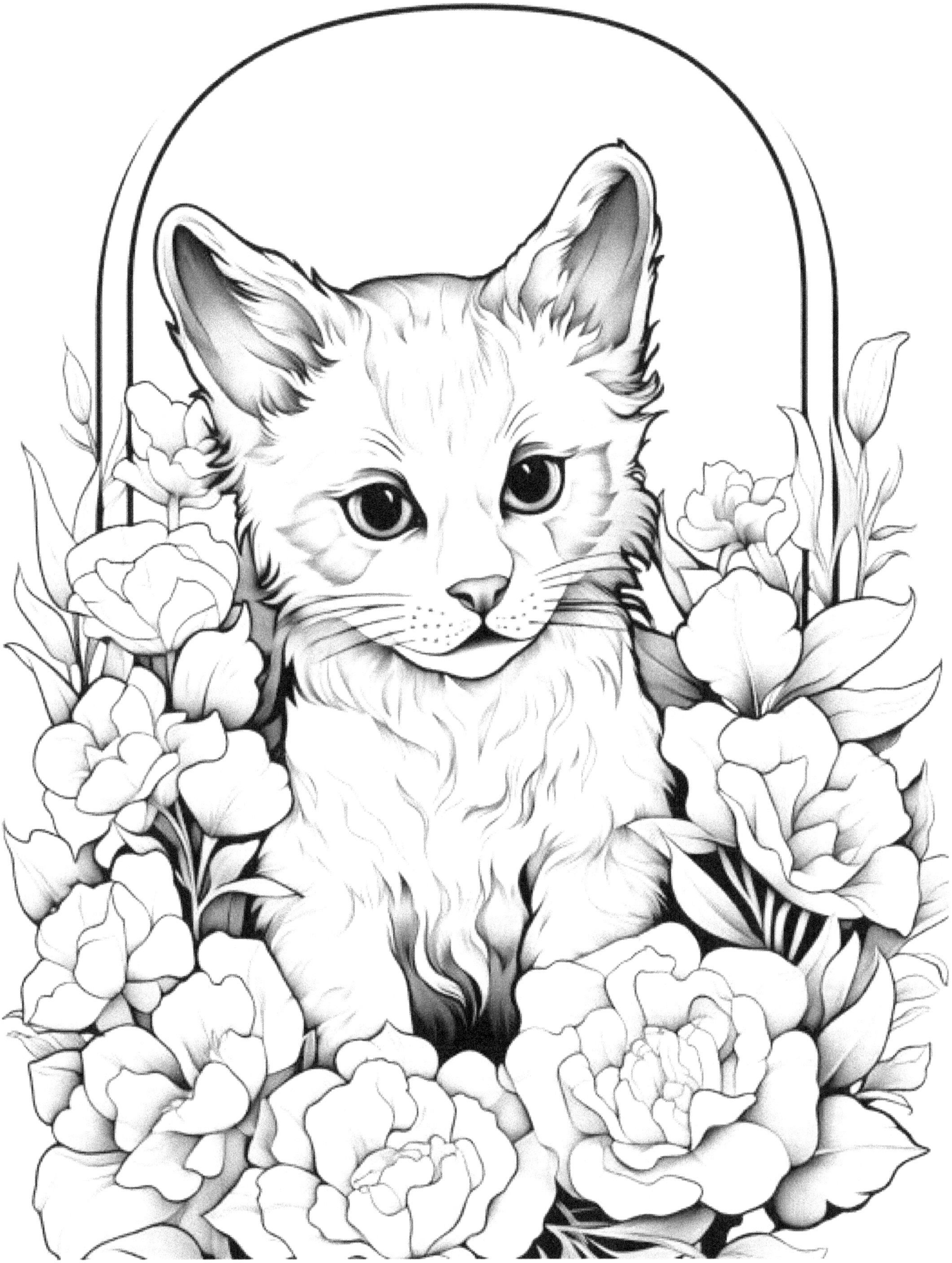

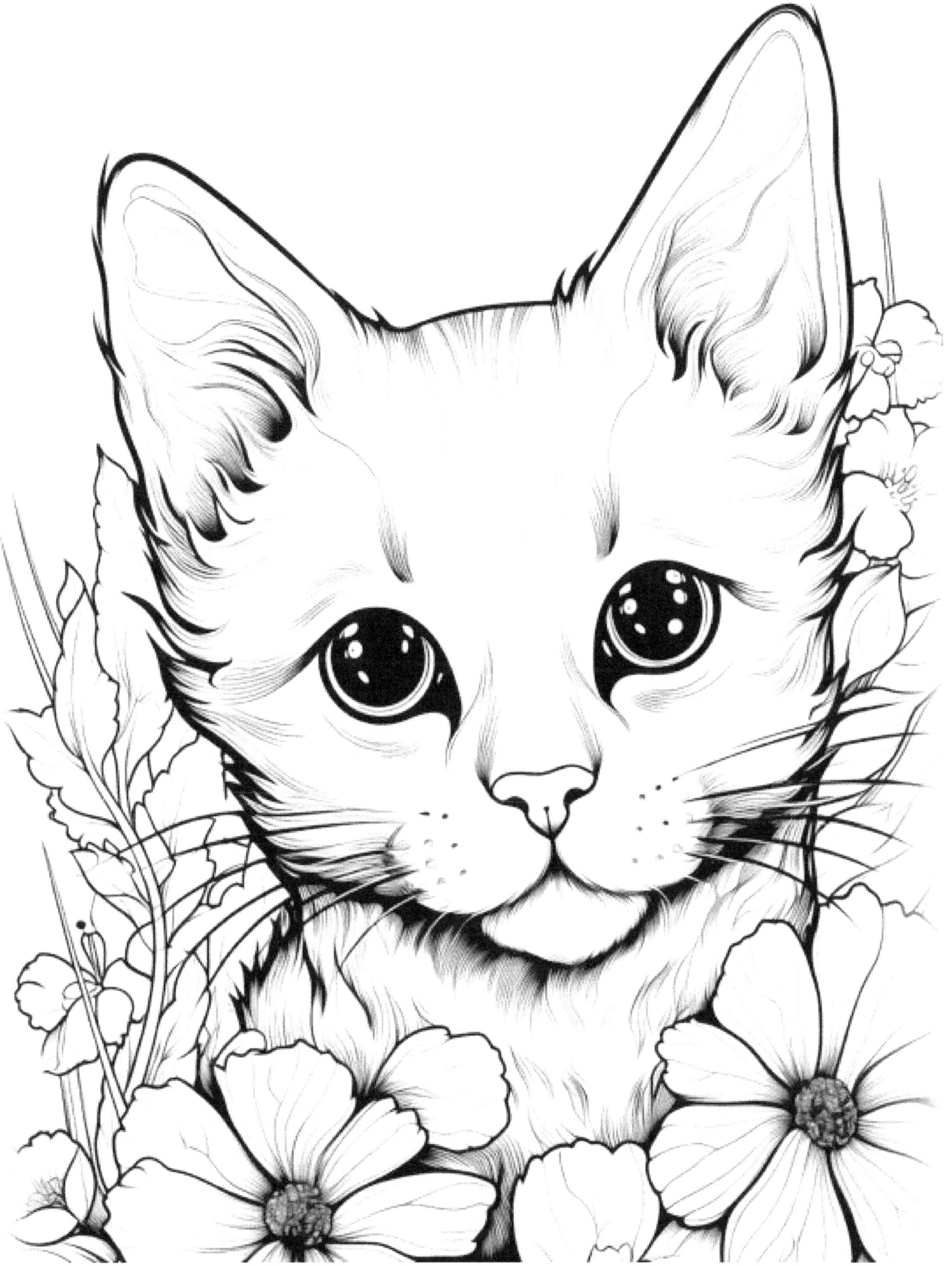

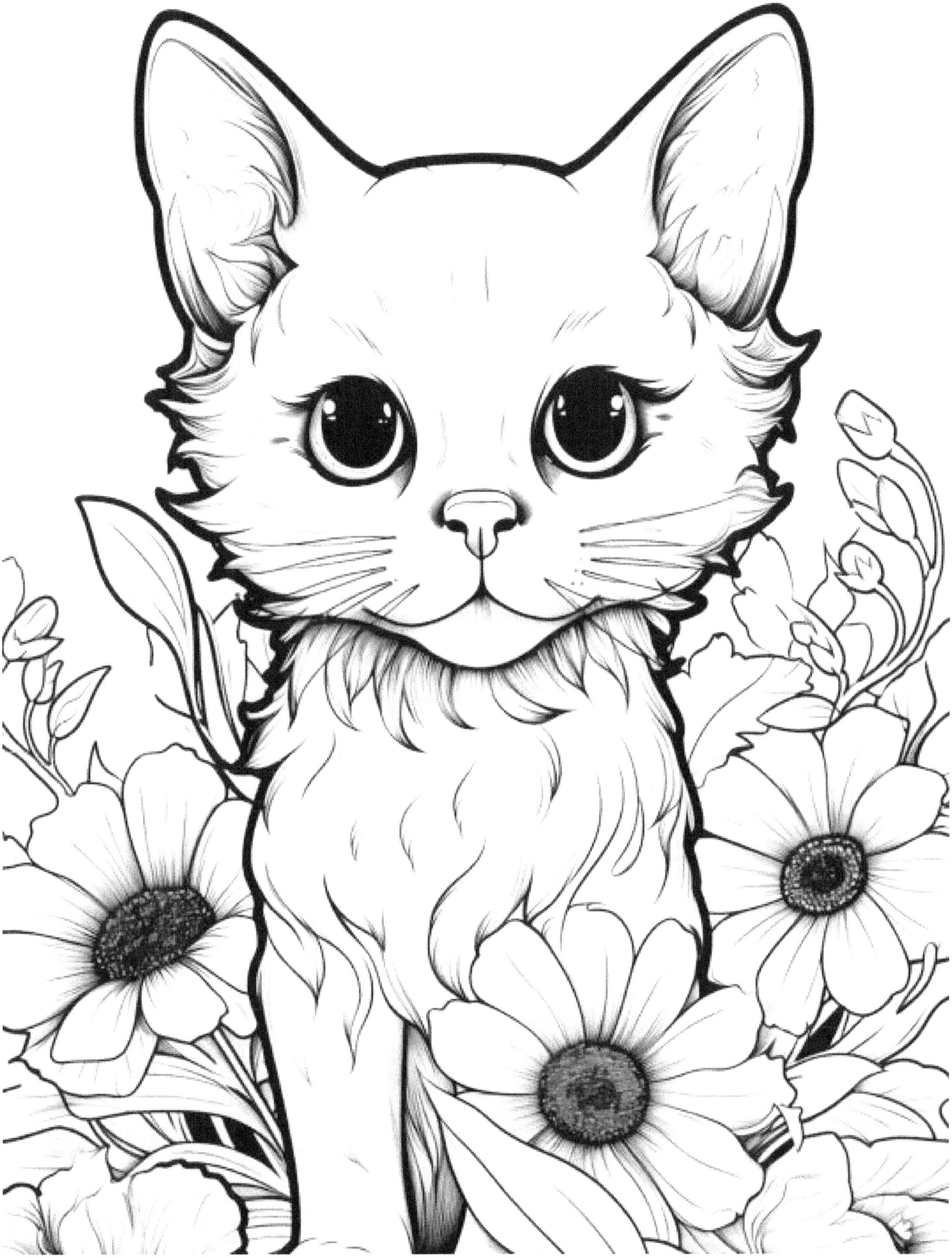

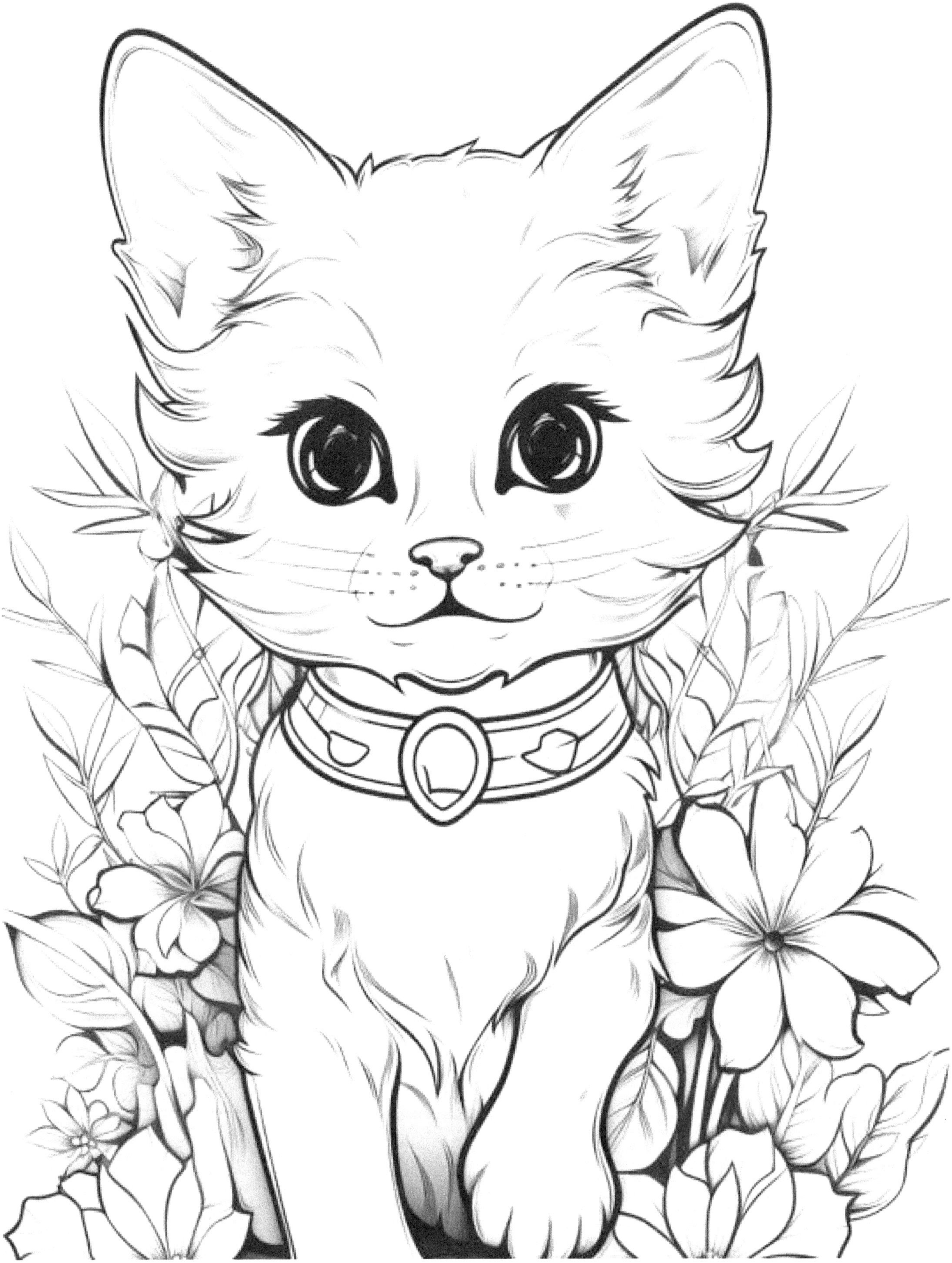

www.ingramcontent.com/pod-product-compliance
Lightning Source LLC
Chambersburg PA
CBHW082137290526
45794CB00008B/3072
9798864814260